SMALL
SPACE
DESIGN
□

SMALL SPACE DESIGN

□

REMODELING APARTMENTS FOR MULTIPLE USES

□

PAUL SHAFER
and
JEAN WEINER

 VAN NOSTRAND REINHOLD COMPANY

Copyright © 1984 by Van Nostrand Reinhold Company
Library of Congress Catalog Card Number 84—2391
ISBN 0—442—29323—2

Printed in the United States of America
Designed by Beth Tondreau
Photographs by Brian Lafferty

Published by Van Nostrand Reinhold Company Inc.
135 West 50th Street
New York, New York 10020

Van Nostrand Reinhold Company Limited
Molly Millars Lane
Wokingham, Berkshire RG11 2PY, England

Van Nostrand Reinhold
480 La Trobe Street
Melbourne, Victoria 3000, Australia

Macmillan of Canada
Division of Gage Publishing Limited
164 Commander Boulevard
Agincourt, Ontario M1S 3C7, Canada

16 15 14 13 12 11 10 9 8 7 6 5 4 3 2 1

Library of Congress Cataloging in Publication Data

Shafer, Paul, 1948—
  Small space design.

  Includes index.
  1. Apartments—Remodeling for other use. I. Weiner,
Jean, 1950—   . II. Title.
NA7860.S53 1984   728.3'14   84—2391
ISBN 0—442—29323—2

CONTENTS

PREFACE and ACKNOWLEDGMENTS

When we started Cobuild Design Associates, we worked on the idea that many people in urban environments live in small and often unattractively laid-out apartments. They are in great need of help to make these places livable, both functionally and aesthetically. Based in New York, we knew of many people with active lives and limited space. We combined our experience in theater lighting and set design with our training in architecture and interior design to solve problems that our friends and then their friends brought to us. More people found out about our work through articles, especially one written by Suzanne Slesin in the Home Section of *The New York Times*.

The projects in this book show a selection of designs for clients, executed within the confines of the existing walls—none of these designs involved altering the apartment itself. Each project was designed to meet an individual's requirements, but each contains ideas that can be used in a wide variety of other spaces. First, each project illustrates space-saving ways to meet practical needs. Second, and much more important, the projects show how the solutions to these problems can transform a space into a room that is a treat to walk into. Each of these rooms represents a triumph of the owner in a city where one of the many challenges faced is often one's own apartment.

In our early projects, we concentrated on individual space-saving approaches within the rooms, designing built-in storage, redoing closets, or improving kitchen shelving. This book gives an idea of the evolving process of our designs, which now include total room, apartment, and home design. In the past two years, we have consulted on apartment design to approximately one hundred people. About eighty-five of these projects have been built, and more are in the process of being constructed. Learning about our clients by working on these projects showed us a widespread problem—the need for a new type of interior design. This we see as a result of the new ways in which people live. Although occupying small spaces, they live with more mobility and independence and have more flexibility in their relationships than ever before. The people for whom we designed the projects in this book have impressed us over and over as people who need a space designed for their future as well as their present needs. Our clients want to style their homes the way they style their lives—as efficient, customized vehicles to get them where they want to go.

Often people come to us after they have tried to model their apartments on ideas suited to larger and more expensive homes. Experimentation has shown them that the designs they see in magazines are often geared to people who have very different goals in home design than they do. They realize that they want more from an interior design than a prestigious look alone. They want a design that will give rigorous attention to their individual needs, not an approach which imposes an aesthetic without taking their needs into account.

Designing a space means getting to know the people and getting to know their needs. Often people express these needs in terms of practicalities—a new desk and a separate sleeping area, let's say. Talking with them reveals a more complicated set of needs. For example, the desk may be used to write a musical score for a new movie and the bed area may be for a child who will be spending weekends with a single parent.

In this way the problem begins to take on life. What is it like to write music? What kinds of things does a composer need close at hand? Does the room need to be quiet? What degree of separation is needed; what other facilities are required? Do the individuals involved have different schedules? From this process of getting to know the client we create a three-dimensional design that will help the client accomplish what he or she has set out to do.

Whatever the exact plan, the strong appeal of a designed place is to promote a hopeful feeling, to continue looking toward the future. For example, a writer, having finished his first book, is about to write a second book and wants a study that will make writing more comfortable. A woman with a full-time job and three children also wants to be a painter and needs a place to paint in her apartment. Parents want constructions for their children that will last them from infancy through their teenage years until they leave home. Everyone has future plans in mind, and our designs become a statement of optimism about these plans. Through our designs, we try to make people feel that they can organize their lives the way they want and need to. We give people designs expressing their own optimism about themselves.

We would like to thank: Pat Cox and John Macleod, whose intuition and professional advice started us on our way and helped us more than we could ever thank them for; Lee Kirby, for his expert direction and patience throughout the writing of this book; Brian Lafferty, for his beautiful photographs and enthusiasm; Mike Bray, Marc Rice, Marice Pappo, and all our friends, for their interest and support; Wayne Schrengohst, whose talents were equal to any building challenge we presented him with; Tom Rindge, whose steady hand and good humor through many tense moments make him a friend as well a craftsman; Charles Penn and Howard Levinger, whose hard work and skill transformed many of the drawings in this book into reality; Diana Rolls, for her help in the ups and downs of getting our company going; Paul Burns and Lynn Donovan, for their helpful discussions; Woods Mackintosh and Roger Williams, for their help and encouragement with our work; Robin Tobin and Gina Porcelli, whose energy and good spirits in the office were invaluable during hectic days; Clark Kellogg, for his insights, and Ellen Jacobs, for her help with publicity beyond the call of duty; Ruth Ann, Jerry, and Megan, for their understanding and trust which meant so much to us; and above all, our thanks to our clients, whose enthusiasm made designing their spaces fun and exciting. Special thanks to Don and Jo, Stephanie and Lois, Marisa and Bob, Maxine and Paul, Pamela, Lonnie, Eulogio, and Steven.

INTRODUCTION

Our clients lead busy, demanding lives in areas where space is precious. They are people whose lives are changing—they may be planning to have a child, to start a business at home, to develop a hobby, or to make their homes more comfortable for entertaining friends. Our designs aim at meeting such complex needs. In a practical sense, the most common demand is that the same space must function in several ways. For example, a writer's or an artist's small apartment may need to be an office and workshop during the day, a dining room in the evening, and a place to exhibit work and to entertain at night. In an aesthetic sense, people want to make their homes beautiful. They want a space that in form, color, and detail provides a comfortable respite from the stress of city living. In an apartment designed to serve all these functions, a person can pursue new interests without sacrificing old pleasures.

The space crunch

The typical urban client moved several years ago into a small apartment and planned to move again when space dictated. In the meantime, rental and purchase costs increased astronomically, making it difficult if not impossible to move. This situation puts extreme demands on limited space. Children need room to play but often are given the smallest room in the apartment. Adults need a place for their social lives and for work or hobbies. And there is the constant problem of storage for books, toys, old tax records, and off-season clothes.

This space crunch results in the need to use every inch of space with maximum efficiency. Old spaces must be adapted to new purposes. A bedroom may double as a living room, a dining room as a bedroom, or a living room as an office. The designs in this book were developed because people needed new, more space-intensive planning to adapt their existing space to new uses.

Environment

Most of the designs in this book involved spaces difficult to use for any purpose. Some rooms were very small, such as maids' rooms (small rooms near the kitchen, formerly used for servants) and dining alcoves. Some were badly proportioned, with low ceilings or oddly placed windows. Some had little natural light, while in others control of light was critical. Whatever the problems, the inhabitants wanted to turn aesthetically limited spaces into pleasant surroundings. For example, Don and Jo have a duplex apartment in a brownstone, two rooms of which are located in what used to be the cellar. The space was essentially unusable, with a very low ceiling and minimal natural light. They commissioned us to reorganize the downstairs area into a bedroom suite, with an office/guest room upstairs. This problem was typical because, beyond all the space-saving "tricks" (storage under the stairs, built-in shelves, and a combination closet/simulated window), the design had to create a beautiful space from very rough raw material. The changes had to be visually dramatic without involving demolition, major construction, or an impossible budget. Not only do Don and Jo now enjoy increased privacy and comfort, but the admiration of their friends is a constant source of pleasure.

Limitations of traditional solutions

Many clients have already tried to solve their design problems on their own with furniture bought in stores. But they found that their problem was an organizational one that went beyond the function of separate pieces of furniture. One family bought three successive couches, hoping to find one that would make the room feel right, but none of them worked. The solution had to take into consideration the unique problems of the entire space along with the individual requirements. For example, the choice of a couch was only one problem. The family also needed a separate kitchen, a dining area, and space for books and pottery display. In addition, the windows looked out on a sunless courtyard, and the entrance to the room was through a long, narrow hallway. We based our design on an overview of all these problems and let the seating emerge from the overall design. This approach helped the family obtain everything they wanted from their home and saved money and time wasted on piecemeal efforts.

Such solutions require a unique design geared to the individual situation. There are few products available in stores that will help, and comprehensive designs for intensive space use are rarely published. One of the reasons that the designs in this book came about was the lack of preexisting solutions on which people could base their planning.

These designs are a response to a common need—that people want an apartment that is unique to their individual aesthetic and practical problems. As the designs emerged, the spaces became original entities, units more elegantly adapted to the individual than most clients ever imagined possible. Barbara telephoned us after she had studied the design drawings for a couple of days. "I couldn't believe that you knew me so well," she said. "You thought more about what I needed than I did myself."

Design approach

The traditional way to make a small apartment work is to hide everything—to make the space look empty. The approach in the designs shown here is exactly the opposite. The complexity of the space requirements becomes the framework of the design, while an open feeling and free wall space remain priorities.

In creating the design framework to meet both practical and aesthetic needs, we reshape the space in a way that at first may feel unconventional or unfamiliar to the client. Lonnie describes his room affectionately to his friends as "looking like a newsstand." Another design became known, during construction, as the "tree house," because of its cantilevered platforms. The designs often create a new aesthetic that comes as a relief to the client—the old use of the space was inhibiting or depressing or just didn't work.

Each design responds as individually to the place as it does to the person. This means working with existing natural light, view, proportions of the room, and other features, such as fireplaces, oversize doors, and elaborate moldings. Many apartments have further restrictions, such as structural columns and steam radiators protruding into a room. We deal with these problems by creating a "subarchitecture" within the space. We design elements that change the volume and the shape of the room. If it feels too long and narrow, perhaps an overhead element can divide the room visually. Or in a room that feels too square and boxlike, we might design a diagonal unit in one corner. We create these new shapes from practical elements. The overhead structure may be a shelf for oversize books; the diagonal unit may be a closet. There are no hard and fast rules for arriving at a solution, but the effect is to change the shape and feeling of the room, creating an architecture tailored to the actual use the room will be put to.

There is great satisfaction in originating a design that shows a client that he or she can live in the way desired in a particular apartment. Often, it is the first time the client realizes that a space, which before may have been thought of as an enemy, can be made to fit the individual. Instead of feeling that his or her life must be organized around the apartment, the client sees that the apartment can be organized around the person's life-style.

Design process

Many clients are new to interior design. They are often ambivalent about beginning the project. Many have never worked with a designer. The process of moving from the initial telephone call to the completed project varies slightly depending on the individual project, but the basic steps are similar.

The first contact with a client is usually over the telephone. The conversation can range from a calm inquiry about procedure to a desperate plea for help. After getting an idea of the problem involved, we invite the prospective client to come to our office and see our work through our models, photographs, and drawings. The next step is to go to the apartment to see the problem firsthand. This visit is the main information-gathering step. Just the fact that the designer is coming encourages people to think about what they want. Since the apartment may now be someone else's "problem," they let themselves think more freely. Instead of deciding that the problem can't be solved, they start to think about what could be different, about everything they would like to change. Clients often have clippings and pictures to illustrate what they would like. This consultation is a chance to get to know the person and to begin to clarify and to read between the lines as to what a client wants and expects.

Next, the apartment is measured thoroughly and the client's possessions are cataloged—how much drawer space, how much closet space, how many books. We then develop a design that integrates all the information we have accumulated. The design is expressed in concept drawings, including three-dimensional representations—a perspective sketch, an axonometric drawing, or sometimes a model. When the drawings are ready, we meet with the client again and present our ideas.

After the drawings are presented, some people want to get started right away; some deliberate over major decisions. When Steven saw our design for his office/bedroom, he was at first dubious about the central of three columns that separated the areas of the room. We left him the model, in which the controversial column was made removable, so he could study it. Once all the final decisions have been made and the drawings approved, work is ready to begin.

Starting construction

The day work starts is a traumatic one, due to the realization that the space is really going to change. A roomful of cabinets waiting to be installed is an indisputable fact. One client left the room abruptly as the carpenters started to install her new home office and didn't come back until several hours later. We try to check every detail before the construction starts but every so often something is missed. The day before work was to start on one job, the client called with a problem. The opening to the cats' hidden litterbox was too small. The crisis was averted by extending the cabinet two inches so that the extraordinarily plump cats could fit with ease.

As we follow the project through construction, there are always difficult moments. As the elements are put into place, it may still be difficult to see what the finished product will be like. Sometimes the events that are visually the most important, such as painting or installing the window treatment, take place at the very end. Through these ups and downs, jobs get done, and the space is ready to be reoccupied by its owner. Richard scarcely let the carpenter finish the steps to his new second level bedroom before he had his mattress set up, pictures hung, and carpet fastened down. Lonnie, an actor, walked around his apartment, which had been equipped with a motorized loft bed/sofa. He approached it like an actor who was on a set for the first time, asking instructions on how to operate the bed and checking out the different areas of his "stage." Another client immediately unpacked his books and lovingly put them in order using the Dewey decimal system.

Construction process

How a project is executed depends on the type and extent of the work involved. If several trades are involved, such as plastering, plumbing, and wiring, a general contractor can be hired. A general contractor takes charge of hiring and coordinating the individual workers. On less complicated jobs, a carpenter and a painter can be hired separately, with the designer or the client coordinating the work. A few clients even undertake part of the work themselves, such as painting the room or the finished cabinets.

The designs in this book were built using a combination of units prepared in a shop, with pieces cut and fit on location. Before installation of the woodworking the electrical work, such as moving switches and installing new outlets, was completed. Then the rooms were painted. With this work done, the new units could be moved in and assembled. A few of the projects required special rigging skills when moving or motorized parts were involved. These projects were a lot of fun, but for reasons of safety, no one should undertake such a project without professional advice.

Materials

The choice of materials can be made toward the end of the design process, when conflicting space and financial demands have been reconciled into a three-dimensional solution. One basic material is birch-veneer plywood. It is easily available, and many woodworking shops are equipped to work with it. Birch-veneer plywood provides a good surface for painting and is relatively inexpensive. Details such as shaped railings and cantilevered sections are also more easily constructed with plywood.

On most of the projects in this book, new construction was painted to match the walls of the room. This made new pieces less dominant and helped them to blend in with the rest of the room. Sometimes parts such as a shelf unit or a desk top were left in natural wood with a polyurethane finish. A few projects were left almost entirely in natural wood.

Details

Detailing was kept simple. Corners and edges were rounded for safety, especially in a child's room. Edges that receive a lot of wear— the front edge of a step, for example— were made of hardwood. If different units were located next to each other, a small space, a reveal, was left between them to visually break the mass of adjoining units. Horizontal surfaces, such as desk tops and counters, were usually made of formica, but a piece of good veneer plywood with a natural finish was sometimes used, depending on the look of the project and on the client's taste. Handles on drawers and doors were either grooves cut into the edges of the wood itself or metal in a brass or chrome finish. Cabinet doors and lift-up tops were hinged with continuous or concealed hinges.

Colors

The background color used in most of these projects was a warm off-white. The rest of the color scheme was provided by upholstery, bedspreads, and other personal possessions. This unobtrusive use of color allows people more choice in selecting or later changing the accessories in the room.

Lighting

The projects shown in this book utilize three types of lighting. Overall light is provided by placing one or more fixtures to reflect light off the ceiling or out of the corners of the room. Lights for specific uses, such as reading in bed, highlighting a piece of art, or working at a desk are a second type. A third type is lighting to enhance the spatial design. These lights define an area or emphasize the separation between areas. Sometimes lights will do double duty, as when a fixture over a desk area also provides light for working at the desk. The general lighting, the specific lighting, and the area-definition lighting are all controlled separately by switches or dimmers. This allows a wide variety of illumination, according to the needs and moods of the occupant. The fixtures used in the projects in this book were inexpensive, mostly under $30 and many considerably less. Often general lighting was provided by one or two 150-watt bulbs in porcelain sockets, concealed in a bookcase or some other element in the room. They are above eye level and 18 to 24 inches below the ceiling. The specific-use lights were often a cylinder light on a swivel base with a 50-watt reflector spotlight. Sometimes we used a desk lamp with a spring and arm arrangement, which allows for a good deal of flexibility in adjustment. The lighting for area definition was built into space-defining elements, such as an overhead frame or a "trough" running around or across the room. These were very small fixtures, such as miniature track lights, small recessed fixtures, or specially constructed strings of lights resembling Christmas-tree lights. For all three types of lights, the emphasis was on the effect on the appearance and use of the room, not on the appearance of the fixtures themselves, since they were often concealed.

A PLACE OF ONE'S OWN

☐

Many clients live alone—in a studio apartment, one-bedroom apartment, or loft. They want the whole space, however big or small, to be organized for their own personal needs. Since these clients have all kinds of hobbies, friends, and tastes, each design is different, but the goal is always the same: to accommodate the personality and activities of the client in his or her own apartment.

Some of the projects are quite simple; some are more complex. Eulogio, in his one-bedroom apartment, needed a desk area and an entertainment center to go with already existing seating. He also needed a bed, bookshelves, and some storage for clothes. This project involved designing a basic setup to make his apartment work for him, keeping costs as low as possible. Susie had a loft on Twenty-third Street, in Manhattan, where she had enough room but needed something visually dramatic that would leave enough wall space for painting on large canvases. And she wanted a sleeping area that was separated from the rest of the space. Barbara needed several rooms fitted into her studio apartment: a living room, a bedroom, a study, and a dining room. Each person's individual demand on space was very different, and as a result each design is unique to that person and place. But each design also contains many ideas that can be applied to a wide variety of situations.

1. Tiny room becomes retreat for writer

With her children away at school, Nancy, a writer, sold her house in Westchester and bought a small two-bedroom apartment on the Upper West Side in Manhattan. Nancy was enthusiastic about living in New York and found that her children shared her enthusiasm. They loved to come to New York, bring their friends, and stay over at her new apartment. Although she looked forward to their visits, she found that she needed a place to work and to have some privacy. Nancy wanted to make the tiny maid's room off her kitchen into a retreat that would also double as an office so that she could turn the rest of the apartment over to her children when they were in town. In her new space she wanted to have peace and quiet to think, write, and sleep. Even though the room was fairly small, Nancy wanted a double bed, a desk, and lots of storage for her files and books so that she could keep them organized and easily accessible. Solution: Every inch of space underneath the bed is transformed into filing and storage space. A desk and additional bookshelves complete the room.

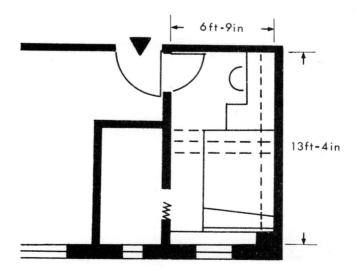

BED AND SHELVES CONTAIN WRITER'S RESEARCH LIBRARY.

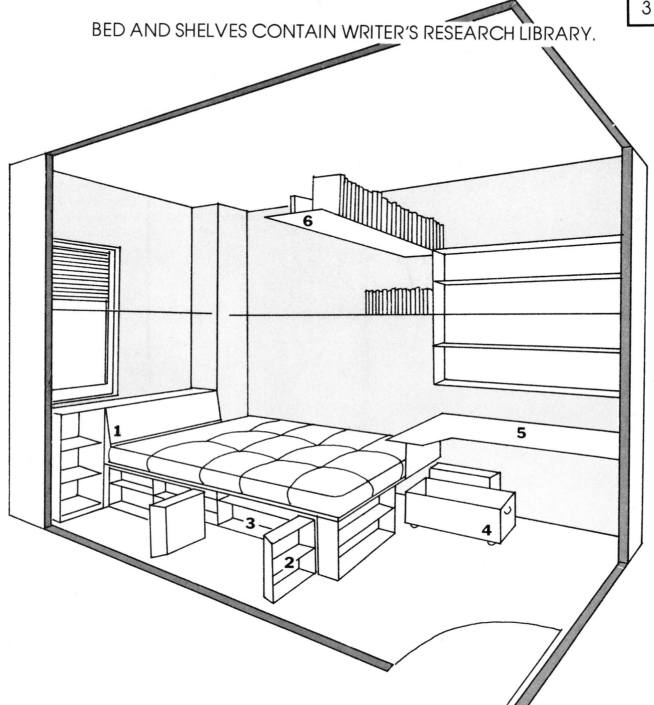

1. Headboard, opens for storage.
2. Hinged bookshelves for access to second row of bookshelves.
3. Second row of bookshelves.
4. Cart for files rolls under bed.
5. Desk with shelves above.
6. Overhead shelf for large books.

2. Work space for an illustrator/writer

Eve, a successful free-lance writer, was beginning to achieve recognition for her illustration work and needed to set up an area at home where she could both write and draw. She was extremely busy and had drawings scattered all over her room; inks and Magic Markers seemed to disappear just when she needed them, and the general disorganization was driving her crazy. Eve had a large corner bedroom in an apartment that she shared with friends. She wanted a work-station unit that would cover only one wall of her room. It needed to include space for her typewriter, lots of bookshelf space, and storage for her writing supplies and finished work. In addition, she needed a large desk surface, pinup space for large drawings, and storage space for artist's supplies, including large pads of paper. Everything needed to be readily accessible with a minimum of set-up time. Solution: The work station consists of bookshelf units with sliding pinup boards grouped above a large desk surface. Additional storage/organizing space is provided by rolling units that fit underneath the desk.

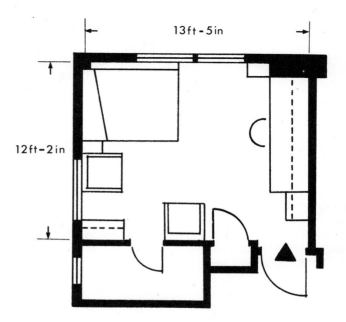

13 ft - 5 in

12 ft - 2 in

CORNER WORK STATION ORGANIZES TWO TYPES OF WORK.

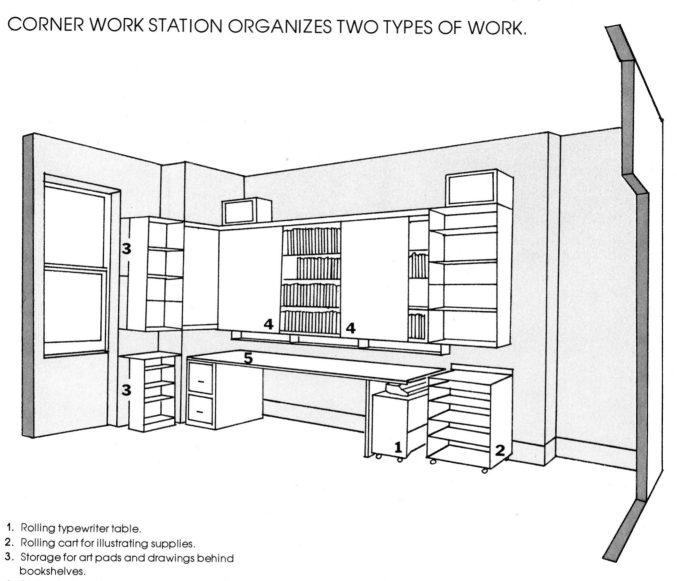

1. Rolling typewriter table.
2. Rolling cart for illustrating supplies.
3. Storage for art pads and drawings behind bookshelves.
4. Sliding bulletin boards.
5. Desk with filing cabinet.

3. Director/computer entrepreneur makes changes on a budget

Eulogio works for a television station and is also developing his interest in computers into a consulting business. To pursue these interests, he needed a work area for his computer and a place for his color television and videotape recorder. Both rooms of his one-bedroom apartment needed work. The only furniture that he wanted to keep was a pair of chairs in the living room. He was on a tight budget so he wanted to set up both rooms with a minimum of expense. Solution: The design for these two rooms is intended to provide the basic elements to live in the apartment—work area, sitting area, and bedroom—using uncomplicated forms and simple cabinetry in order to keep costs down.

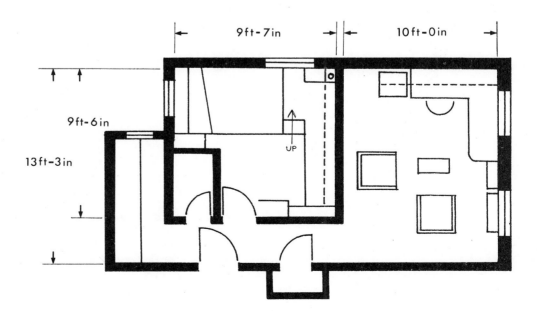

COMPUTER AND VIDEO SETUP COMBINES WORK SPACE WITH LIVING ROOM.

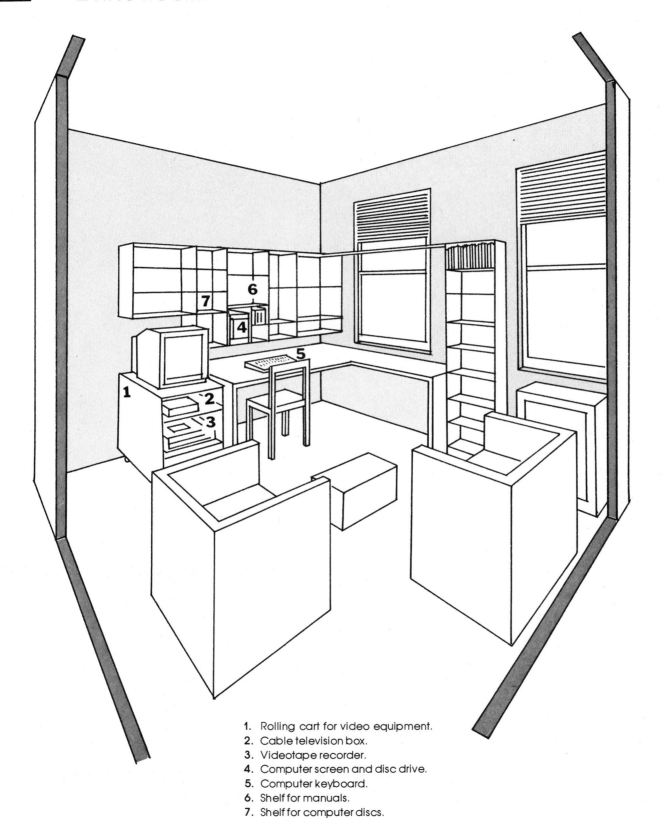

1. Rolling cart for video equipment.
2. Cable television box.
3. Videotape recorder.
4. Computer screen and disc drive.
5. Computer keyboard.
6. Shelf for manuals.
7. Shelf for computer discs.

EIGHT BASICS ORGANIZE THE BEDROOM.

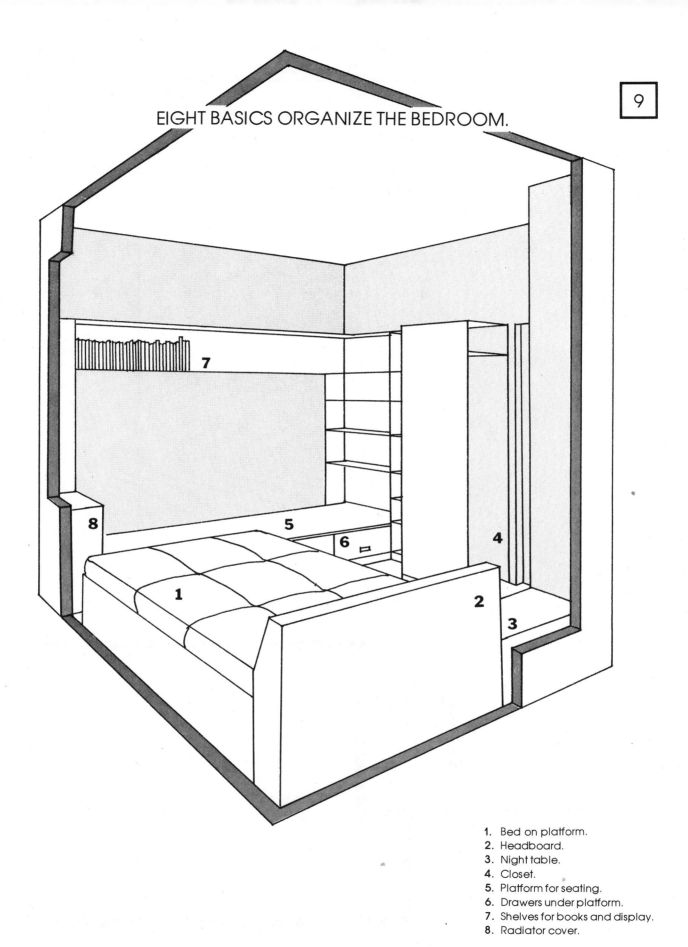

1. Bed on platform.
2. Headboard.
3. Night table.
4. Closet.
5. Platform for seating.
6. Drawers under platform.
7. Shelves for books and display.
8. Radiator cover.

Susie is an active, hardworking young artist living in a small loft while she completes a graduate degree in fine arts. She works with large canvases so she wanted to use every available inch of wall space for painting and to combine everything else she needed into one compact "living unit." She wanted a queen-size bed, a kitchen and dining area, seating, a closet, a desk, bookshelves, and plenty of storage space for paints, pads of paper, and canvas. She also wanted to be able to take the unit with her when she moves since she plans to buy a larger loft of her own once she makes a name for herself. Solution: A stepped, freestanding unit separates sleeping, eating, and kitchen areas. The kitchen is located near a column with plumbing for hookup of kitchen utilities.

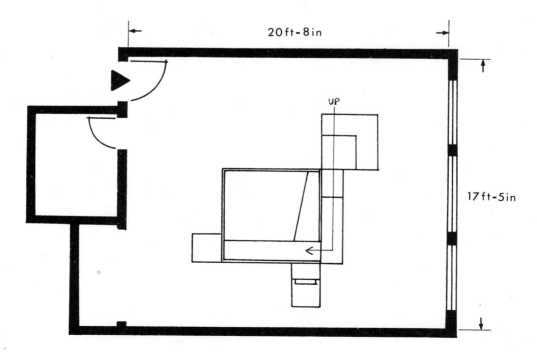

EACH SIDE OF UNIT PERFORMS A DIFFERENT FUNCTION.

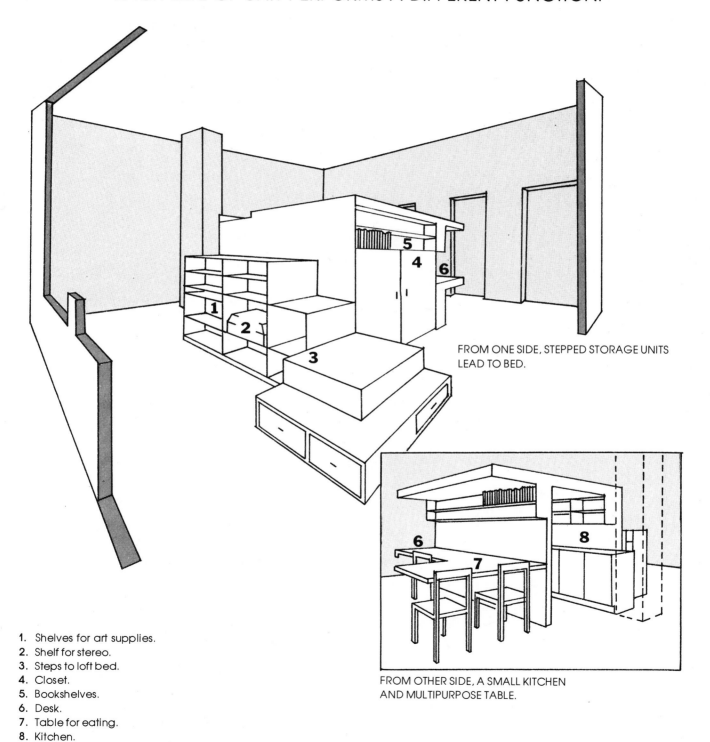

FROM ONE SIDE, STEPPED STORAGE UNITS
LEAD TO BED.

FROM OTHER SIDE, A SMALL KITCHEN
AND MULTIPURPOSE TABLE.

1. Shelves for art supplies.
2. Shelf for stereo.
3. Steps to loft bed.
4. Closet.
5. Bookshelves.
6. Desk.
7. Table for eating.
8. Kitchen.

5. Pied-à-terre for a set designer

Linda is on the road much of the time because of her work as a set designer and keeps only a tiny room in a friend's apartment. Her schedule is usually very hectic, so by the time she gets home in the early hours of the morning she just wants a place to relax, sleep, or have a quiet drink with a friend. All she needed was a small closet; a place for her stereo, some records, and favorite objects; a couple of chairs; and a queen-size bed that wouldn't take over the room. She wanted a simple, uncomplicated room that required a minimum of maintenance yet looked and felt comfortable. Solution: A "floating" bed suspended on metal rods, with steps that form a wall unit for storage, enable Linda to have a "downstairs" living room and an "upstairs" bedroom.

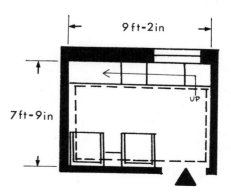

SUSPENDED LOFT BED SALVAGES TINY ROOM.

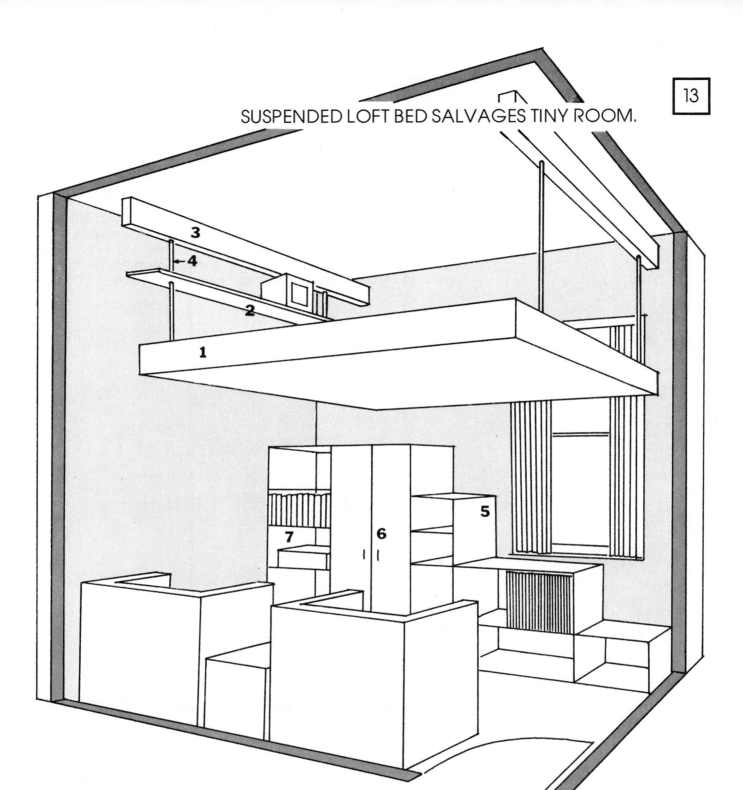

1. Loft bed.
2. Shelf for TV and alarm clock.
3. Overhead supports for loft bed.
4. Metal rods.
5. Steps to loft.
6. Closet.
7. Stereo and bookshelves.

6. Teacher's bedroom doubles as classroom and study

Marc was working on his Ph.D. in education while teaching and tutoring grade-school children privately. He needed to use his tiny bedroom as a classroom and office even though it was barely big enough to hold his queen-size bed and a small desk. He wanted to stay in his present apartment, however, since the location was good for his students and he couldn't afford either a larger apartment or a separate office space until he finished his degree. Solution: A bed that disappears to the ceiling frees the floor space. Cubes on wheels for seating and storage and a desk with a slide-out extension make up the classroom and study.

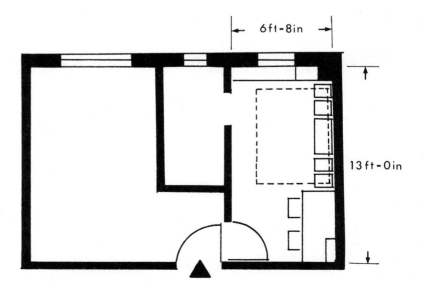

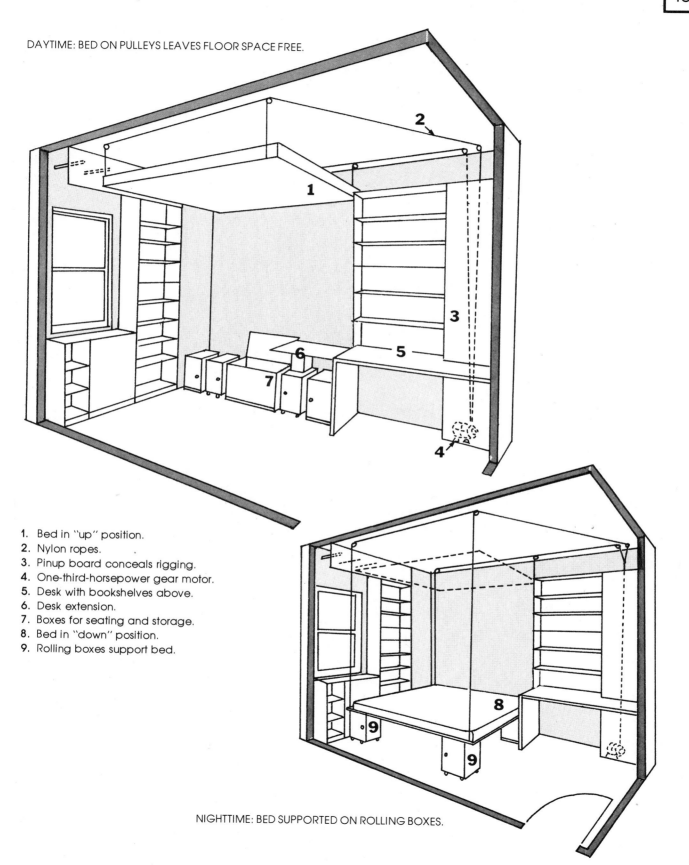

DAYTIME: BED ON PULLEYS LEAVES FLOOR SPACE FREE.

1. Bed in "up" position.
2. Nylon ropes.
3. Pinup board conceals rigging.
4. One-third-horsepower gear motor.
5. Desk with bookshelves above.
6. Desk extension.
7. Boxes for seating and storage.
8. Bed in "down" position.
9. Rolling boxes support bed.

NIGHTTIME: BED SUPPORTED ON ROLLING BOXES.

Dorothy had moved into her studio apartment in the West Village seven years ago when she had just graduated from college and was starting her first job. The apartment was a small, fifth-floor walkup but it had a separate kitchen and it was near a major subway stop. Dorothy had been planning to move to a bigger place once she got established and saved some money. Apartments became hard to find and prices rose so she decided to fix up her present apartment. She wanted to use furniture that was adaptable to other spaces since she was still keeping an eye out for a better apartment. Dorothy liked the idea of multiple functions for each piece, and she wanted everything to look simple, clean, and neat. She wanted a place for all of her clothing and books and was looking forward to reorganizing and purging her apartment of anything extraneous to the design. Solution: Seven movable pieces of furniture along with a closet and shelves provide Dorothy with everything she needs for seating, sleeping, dining, working, and storage.

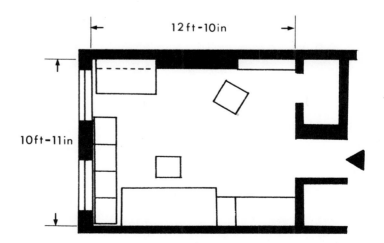

LIVING ROOM/STUDY.

1. Closet.
2. Platform for folded futon makes sofa.
3. Cushioned boxes for seating.
4. Coffee table.
5. Desk with cubbies above.

DINING ROOM.

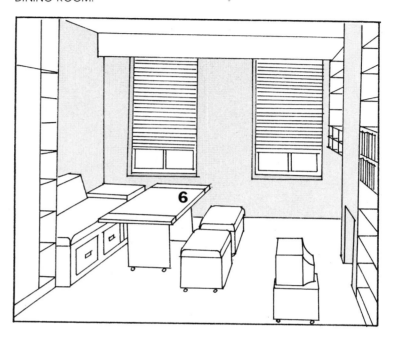

BEDROOM.

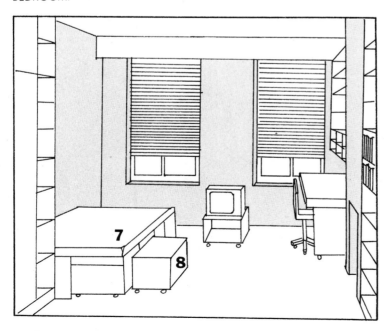

6. Desk rolls out and extends for dining.
7. Futon unfolds onto seating boxes to become bed.
8. Coffee table becomes night table.

8. Word-processor operator starts business at home

Elizabeth had been working for word-processing agencies for several years until she decided to be her own boss, bought a word processor, and set up her own service in her studio apartment. During the day she wanted her apartment to look like a professional office with no hint of a bed, so that clients would not feel uncomfortable when they came to discuss jobs or to pick up work. At night, however, she wanted to be able to "get out of the office" for awhile. Although she hoped to get a slightly bigger apartment in a nearby building, she wanted to start her business right away. Whatever was designed had to work for either apartment and had to be easy to move and reassemble. She needed an area for the word processor that was separated from other activities in the room, as well as storage space for supplies and discs, and an area for people to proofread completed work. She also needed a desk for herself and an area to meet with clients. At night she wanted to have a dining area and a place to chat with friends. And since she was just starting out, she also needed to keep the cost low. Solution: A platform with sides separates the word processor from the rest of the room. The client conference area becomes a bedroom when the bed is rolled out from under the platform, and the desk doubles as dining-room table at night.

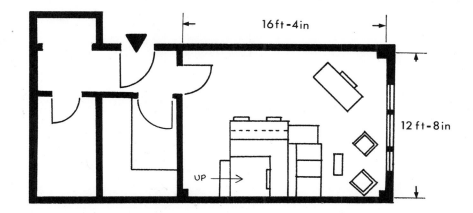

16 ft - 4 in

12 ft - 8 in

UP

PLATFORM/DESK AREA SEPARATES EQUIPMENT FROM THE REST OF THE ROOM.

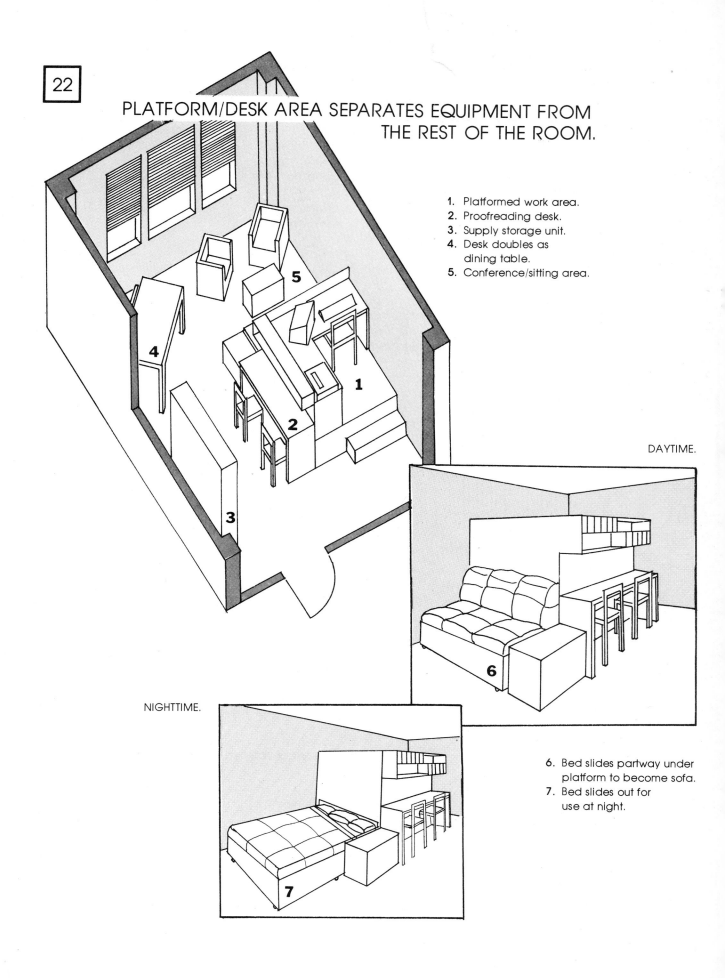

1. Platformed work area.
2. Proofreading desk.
3. Supply storage unit.
4. Desk doubles as dining table.
5. Conference/sitting area.

DAYTIME.

NIGHTTIME.

6. Bed slides partway under platform to become sofa.
7. Bed slides out for use at night.

WORD-PROCESSING STATION IS MADE UP OF SEPARATE, REUSABLE UNITS.

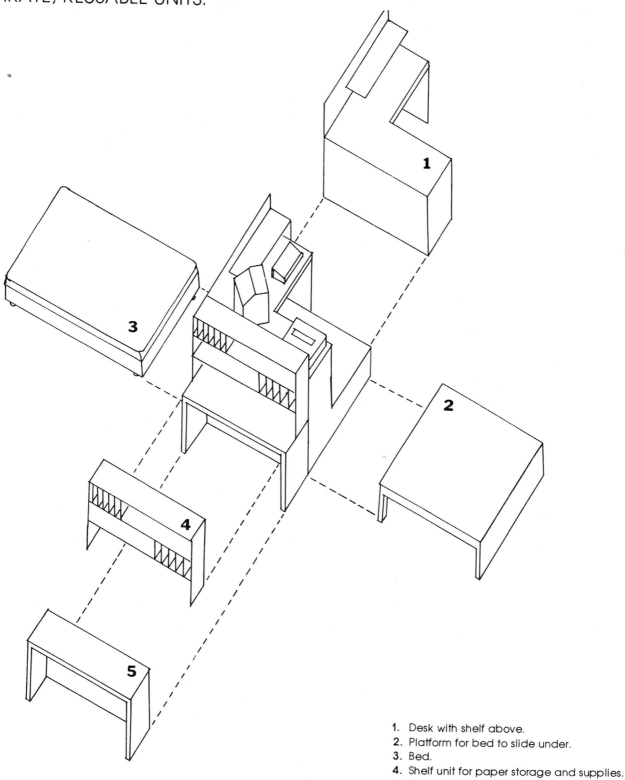

1. Desk with shelf above.
2. Platform for bed to slide under.
3. Bed.
4. Shelf unit for paper storage and supplies.
5. Proofreading desk.

9. Office/showroom doubles as guest room

Dion's business was an unusual one. She was a wine consultant as well as a dealer in jewelry such as charms related to wine. Her business had completely taken over the spare room in her two-bedroom apartment. Although filing cabinets, desks, and bookshelves lined both sides of the room, she still had papers, brochures, and display racks all over the floor. She had her own mental filing system and could locate whatever she wanted, but she needed a part-time assistant and realized that no one else could work or find anything under the existing conditions. She wanted to organize the office, to have room for a wine-tasting table that could also be used to display jewelry, and room for overnight guests. Equally important, she wanted the entire room to feel like a pleasant place where she could enjoy the wonderful view outside, undistracted by the clutter and disorganization inside. Solution: An office area, with a desk that overlooks the view, filing cabinets, bookshelves, and a separate entrance, is located on a platform that separates the office from the rest of the room. Two closets create an entrance while also providing storage. The remaining area of the room can be set up for informal meetings, wine-tasting sessions, or sleeping by rearranging a few pieces of furniture.

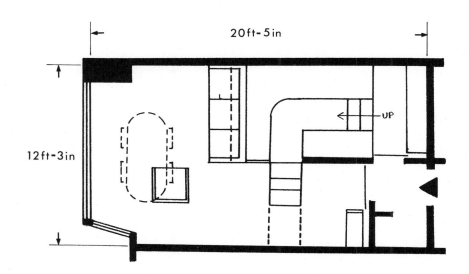

CONFERENCE AREA EASILY ALTERED ACCORDING TO ACTIVITY.

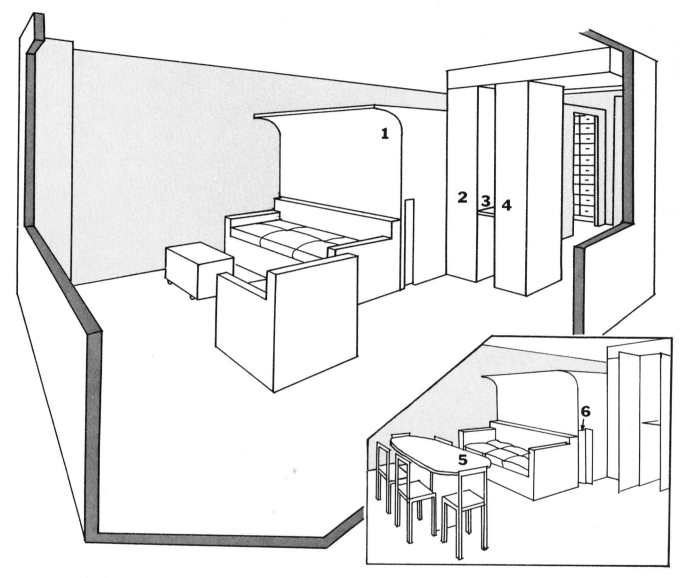

1. Curved divider conceals platformed desk area.
2. Closet.
3. Shelf for display.
4. Closet for folding chairs.
5. Folding table.
6. Storage compartment for folding table.
7. Convertible bed.

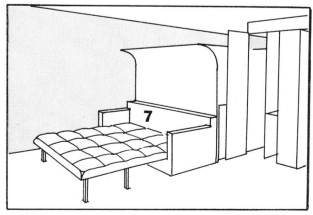

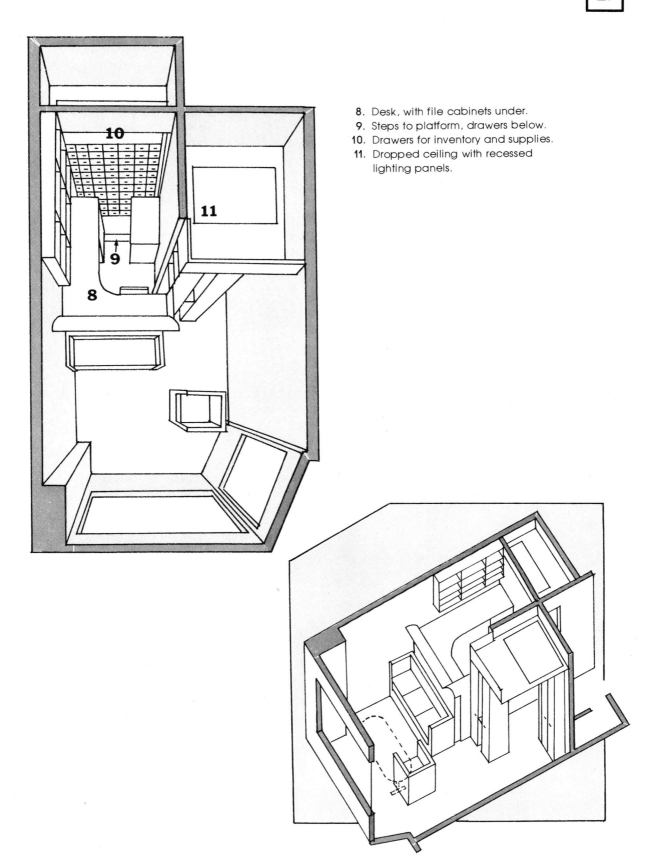

8. Desk, with file cabinets under.
9. Steps to platform, drawers below.
10. Drawers for inventory and supplies.
11. Dropped ceiling with recessed lighting panels.

10. Writer organizes office in bedroom before starting next book

Steven's office had taken over his brownstone bedroom while he was writing his first book. Now that the book was finished, he wanted the piles of papers and books organized and off the floor and a desk that he could spread out on. He wanted a bedroom that was comfortable and that had room for both himself and his large dog. He didn't want to see his bedroom from the entry or the office, and he didn't want to see his office from the bedroom. The rest of his apartment was neat and stylish, and he wanted this room to be the same. Steven also wanted to display the artwork and objects he had collected. He entertains a lot and has many friends, so he wanted the room to function well and be a place to show and talk about. Solution: Three floor-to-ceiling columns control what is seen and unseen from any spot in the room and define a passage through the room. A floor-to-ceiling unit with shelves for books, television, and display separates the bed from the office area. A headboard unit sections off an area for clothing storage and works in conjunction with the columns to hide the bed from the entrance.

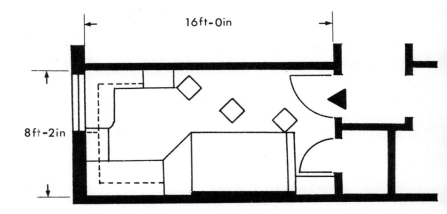

COLUMNS SEPARATE ROOM INTO OFFICE, BEDROOM, AND STORAGE AREA.

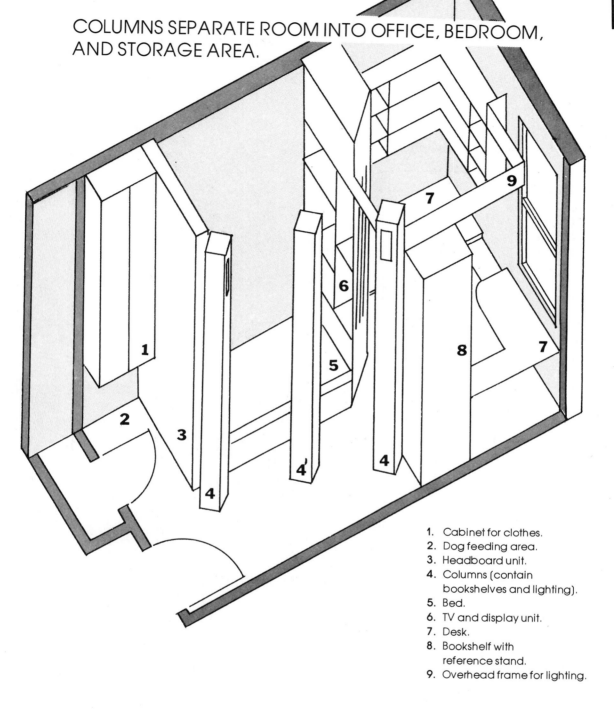

1. Cabinet for clothes.
2. Dog feeding area.
3. Headboard unit.
4. Columns (contain bookshelves and lighting).
5. Bed.
6. TV and display unit.
7. Desk.
8. Bookshelf with reference stand.
9. Overhead frame for lighting.

A VIEW OF COLONNADE FROM THE ENTRANCE.

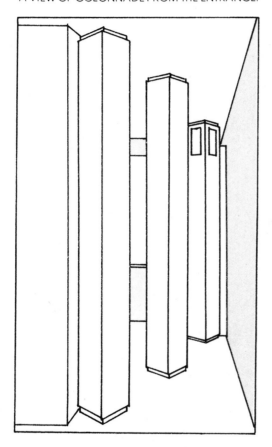

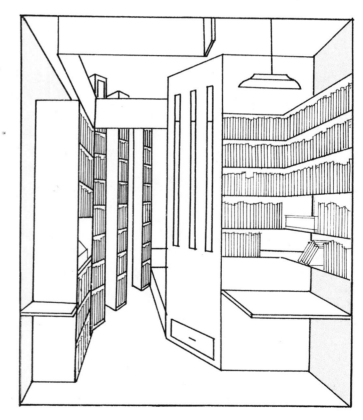

A VIEW OF THE LIBRARY FROM THE OFFICE.

LIGHTING IS CONCEALED WITHIN THE CONSTRUCTION.

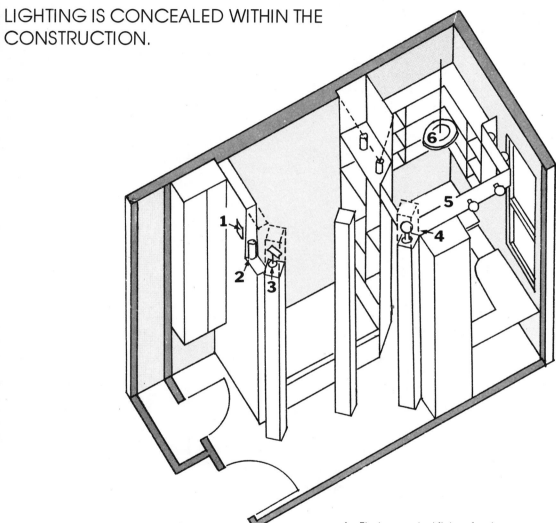

1. Flush-mounted fixture for storage area.
2. Recessed spotlights for display shelves.
3. Concealed spotlight in column to highlight painting.
4. Light in top of column for general illumination.
5. Concealed lights behind frame define office area.
6. Hanging light for desk.

11. Graphic designer remodels living room to include office

Clark had just finished graphic-design school and wanted to set up his first office in the living room of his apartment. He had a beautiful Upper West Side apartment with high ceilings and elaborate architectural molding, wainscotting, and columns. He wanted the office to work with this setting, to remain separate from the living room, and to allow for growth in his business. Clark had been working with an improvised setup in a small room in the back of the apartment, but now he wanted a professional-looking office that he would enjoy having clients see. He wanted the office to be separated from the rest of the apartment to preserve his privacy, yet he didn't want to feel closed off while he was working. He also had a great sense of fun about design that he wanted to explore with his office. Solution: Columns and a pediment echo the existing architecture of the apartment, create an area for the living room, and provide separation and privacy for the office without closing it off. The office is organized to accommodate work areas for three people as well as the different types of storage a designer needs.

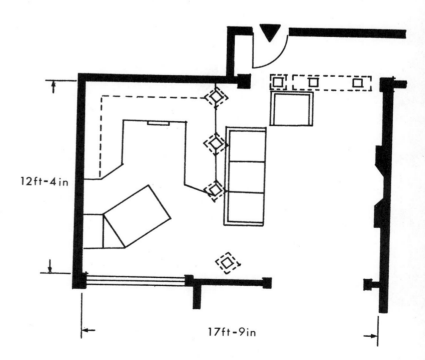

12ft-4in

17ft-9in

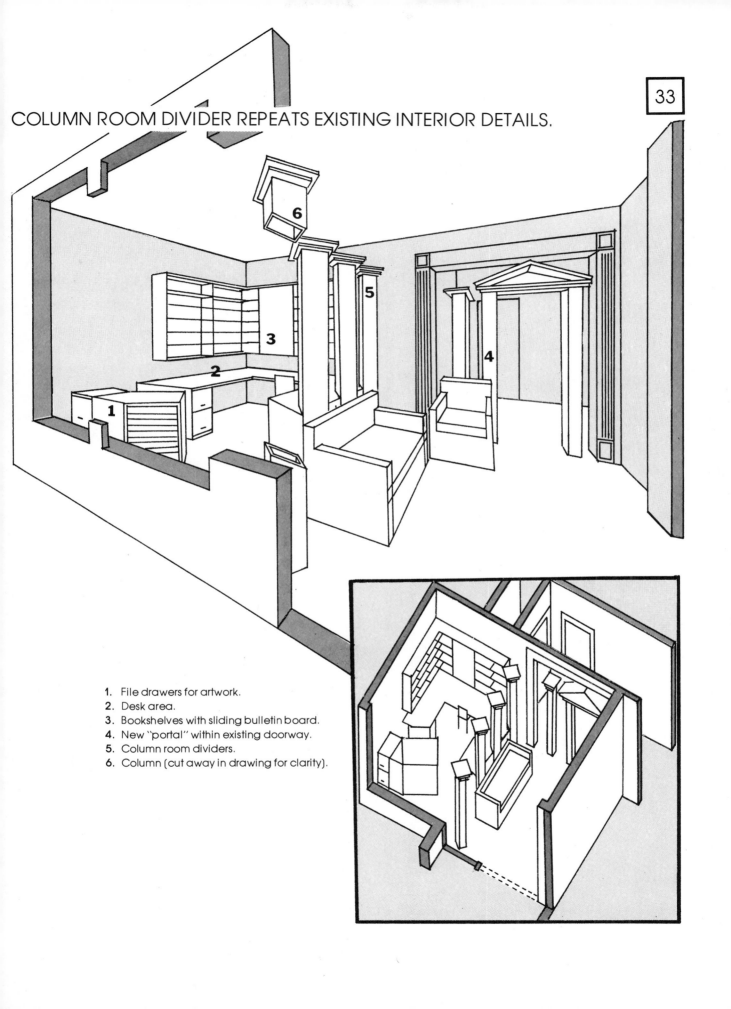

COLUMN ROOM DIVIDER REPEATS EXISTING INTERIOR DETAILS.

1. File drawers for artwork.
2. Desk area.
3. Bookshelves with sliding bulletin board.
4. New "portal" within existing doorway.
5. Column room dividers.
6. Column (cut away in drawing for clarity).

33

12. New look for a stock consultant's studio apartment

Scott wanted to reorganize and improve his tiny studio apartment. He had lived there two years, and now that he was doing well in his stock-consulting position he was ready for a change. He wanted a sense of an entry when he came into the apartment, and he wanted to see a living room rather than a bedroom once he was inside. He wanted a dining area and modern kitchen instead of the kitchen-in-a-closet that he had now. The rest of his requirements were a place for a computer setup, a bar area, and better, more interesting lighting. Above all, his apartment had to look neat and sophisticated. He had started to make some changes himself by buying a Murphy bed unit but then realized he needed help to accomplish all that he wanted. Solution: A small section of curved wall creates separate entrances into the kitchen and living room, defines a dining area, and continues overhead into a diagonal dropped ceiling above an expanded kitchen. Clothes storage, a bar area, and a desk/video-equipment center are contained in built-in units around the room.

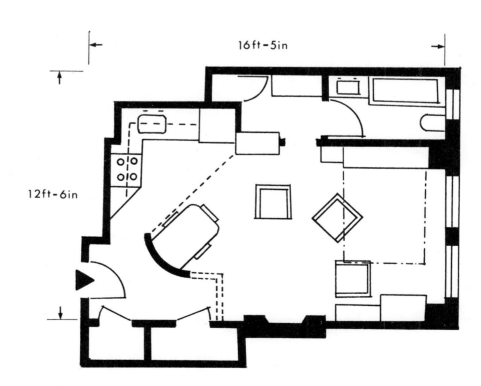

BUILT-IN UNITS FREE FLOOR SPACE FOR FURNITURE AROUND FIREPLACE.

1. Shelf unit for TV and video equipment.
2. Slide-out desk.
3. Fold-down bed.
4. Bar and stereo unit.
5. Fireplace.
6. Dining table built into curved wall.

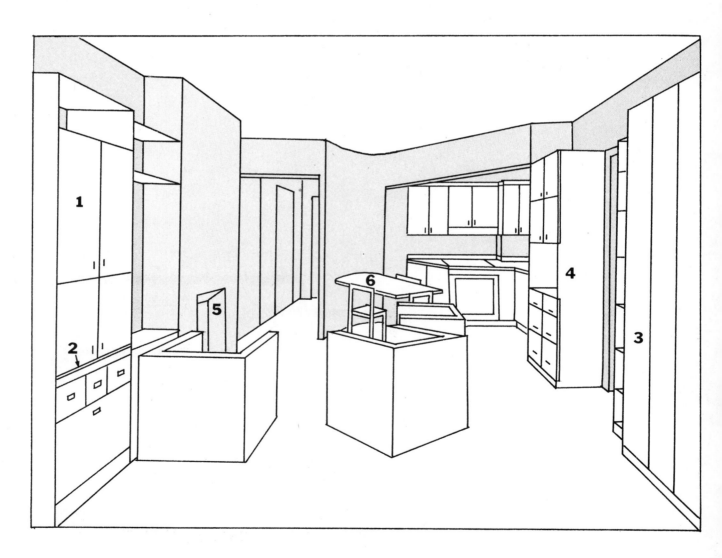

CURVED WALL AND DIAGONAL CEILING DEFINE ENTRANCE,
KITCHEN, AND DINING AREAS.

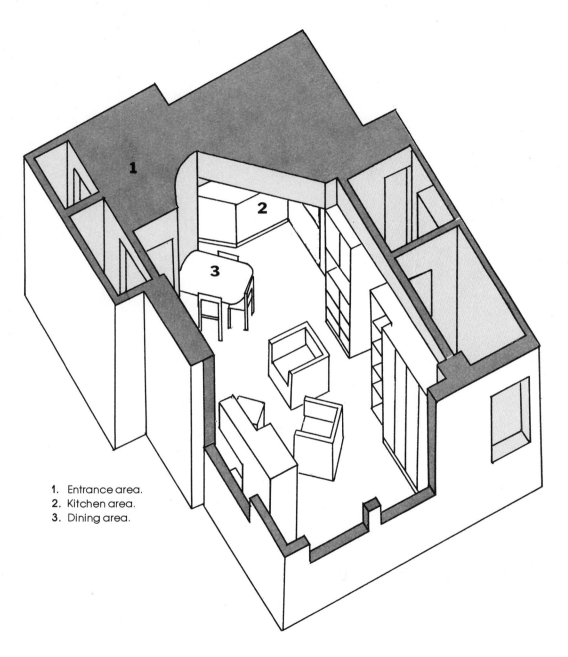

1. Entrance area.
2. Kitchen area.
3. Dining area.

13. Actor sets the stage in his new apartment

Lonnie was very enthusiastic about his first apartment. He had rented a small studio in an old building on a quiet courtyard in Greenwich Village. The apartment was short on space but long on charm. He loved the working fireplace and the view from the windows of the trees and a schoolyard. He worked in theater and film and had many friends who liked to drop by. Music was very important to him, so he needed lots of room for his extensive stereo equipment, record collection, and upright piano. He was moving from a large apartment that he shared with his parents and wanted to bring with him as many of his books and mementos as possible. Since he kept unusual hours and worked hard, he wanted the apartment to be neat and easy to take care of. Lonnie wanted the room to feel more like an actor's studio than a bedroom, so he didn't want his queen-size bed to dominate the room. He wanted the apartment to be a place to come home to, relax, and have fun. Solution: A freestanding two-level structure contains a motorized combination bed and sofa, a fold-down table, and closet space and divides the room into separate areas. The bed tilts up to allow headroom for a sitting area in front of the fireplace. Lights are concealed in various areas around the room. Separate controls make it easy to create whatever mood is desired.

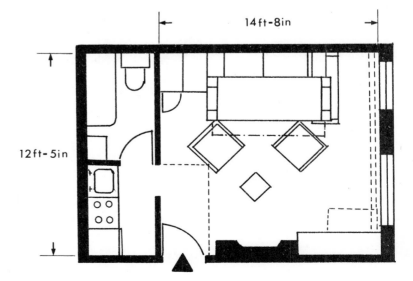

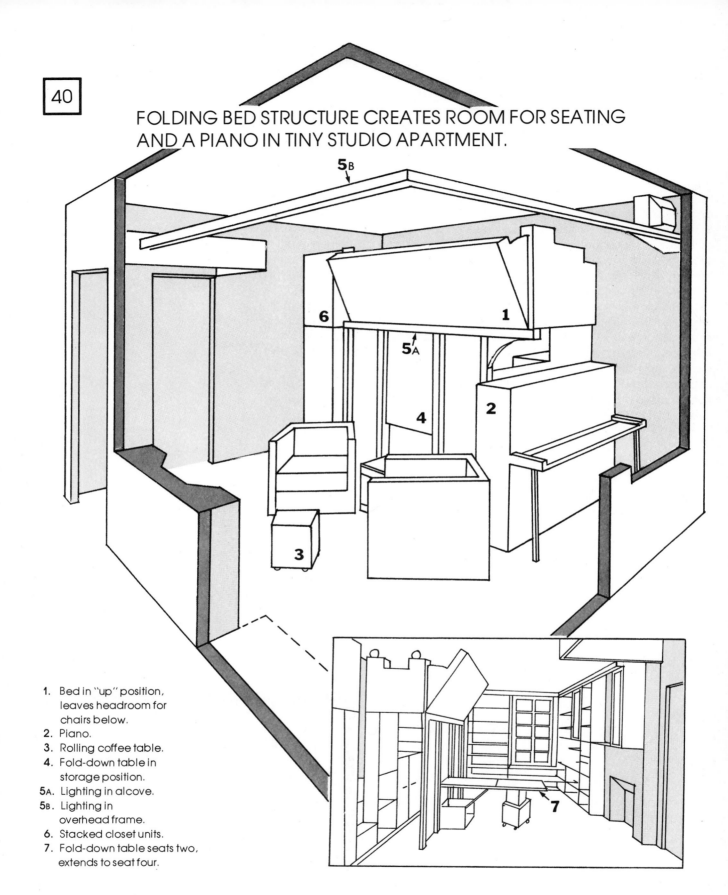

FOLDING BED STRUCTURE CREATES ROOM FOR SEATING AND A PIANO IN TINY STUDIO APARTMENT.

1. Bed in "up" position, leaves headroom for chairs below.
2. Piano.
3. Rolling coffee table.
4. Fold-down table in storage position.
5A. Lighting in alcove.
5B. Lighting in overhead frame.
6. Stacked closet units.
7. Fold-down table seats two, extends to seat four.

BED IN "DOWN" POSITION MAKES SECOND-LEVEL BEDROOM.

8. Bed in "down" position.
9. Steps up to second level.
10. Walk-in closet below bed.
11. Frame with light defines a "foyer."
12. Desk and stereo cabinet.

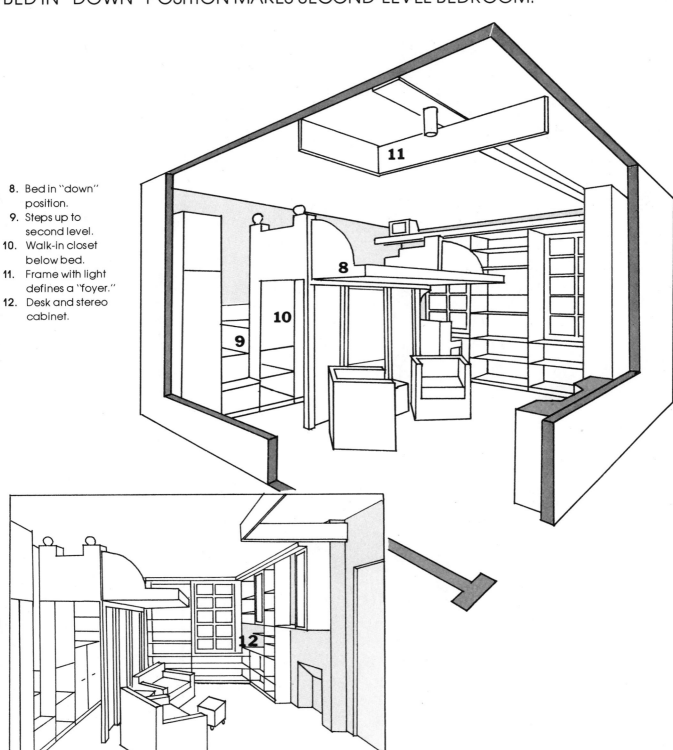

FOLDED UP, THE BED BECOMES A SEPARATE SOFA AREA.

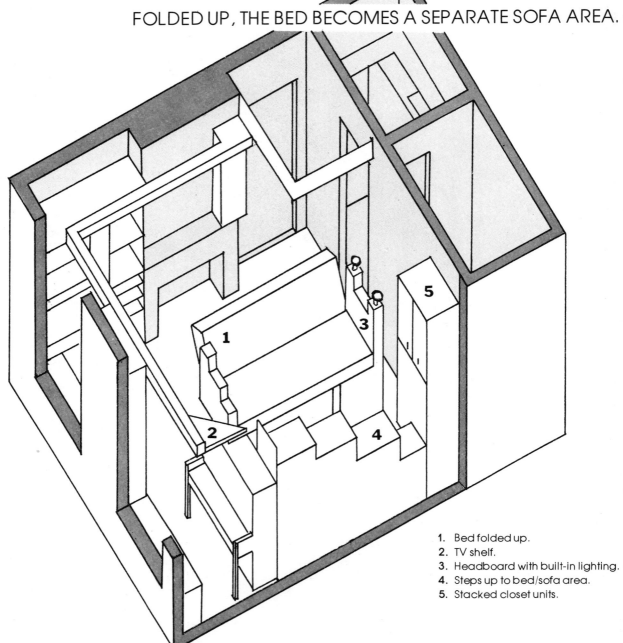

1. Bed folded up.
2. TV shelf.
3. Headboard with built-in lighting.
4. Steps up to bed/sofa area.
5. Stacked closet units.

HOW THE BED WORKS.

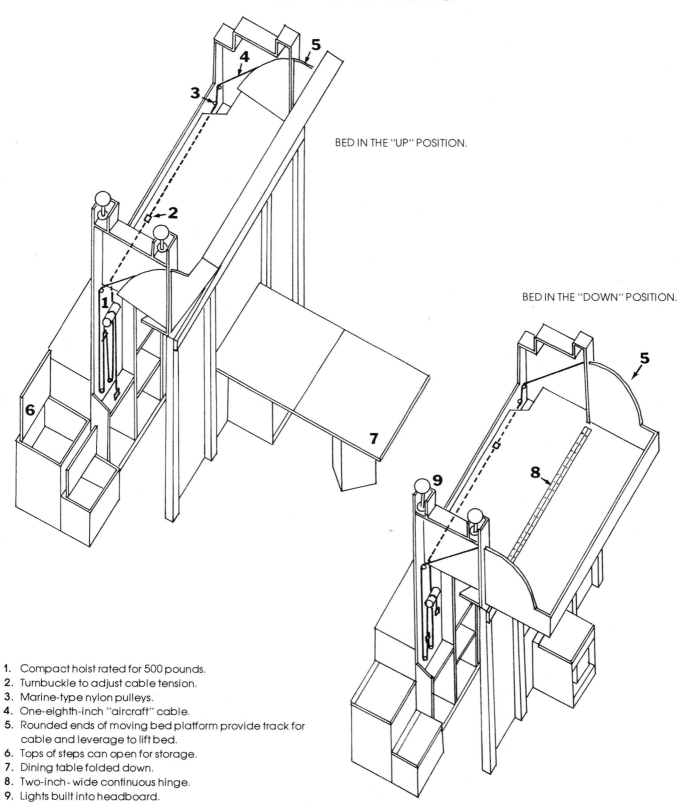

BED IN THE "UP" POSITION.

BED IN THE "DOWN" POSITION.

1. Compact hoist rated for 500 pounds.
2. Turnbuckle to adjust cable tension.
3. Marine-type nylon pulleys.
4. One-eighth-inch "aircraft" cable.
5. Rounded ends of moving bed platform provide track for cable and leverage to lift bed.
6. Tops of steps can open for storage.
7. Dining table folded down.
8. Two-inch-wide continuous hinge.
9. Lights built into headboard.

14. Financial reporter reorganizes her apartment for work and comfort

Barbara had been living in her rent-controlled one-bedroom apartment for sixteen years and her needs had changed. However, she had decided that she wanted to continue living there if she could solve some of the problems of the apartment. The lack of closet space and organization in the apartment was frustrating. She was a writer and worked at home part-time, but her only working surface was a small table in the kitchen that had hardly enough room for her typewriter, let alone her notes and supplies. She liked to travel and had many objects and pictures from her trips but nowhere to display them. In addition, she wanted the apartment to be a comfortable place to entertain friends. Solution: The different planes and shapes of a platform for the piano and bookshelves surrounding the desk divide the room into separate areas with a different mood in each. Storage problems were solved by building a new closet in front of an existing closet, expanding it without any changes that might make the landlord nervous. Overhead frames contain lights that increase the level of light in the apartment. The frames also reinforce the separation between the areas without closing them off.

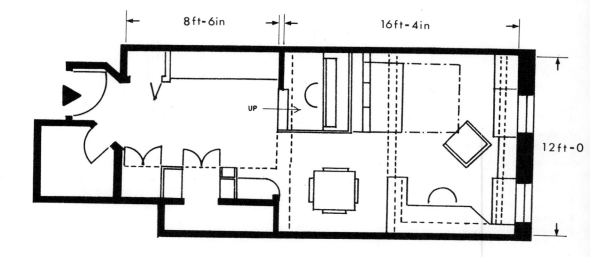

8ft-6in 16ft-4in 12ft-0

STEPPED BOOKSHELVES AND PIANO PLATFORM DIVIDE SPACE.

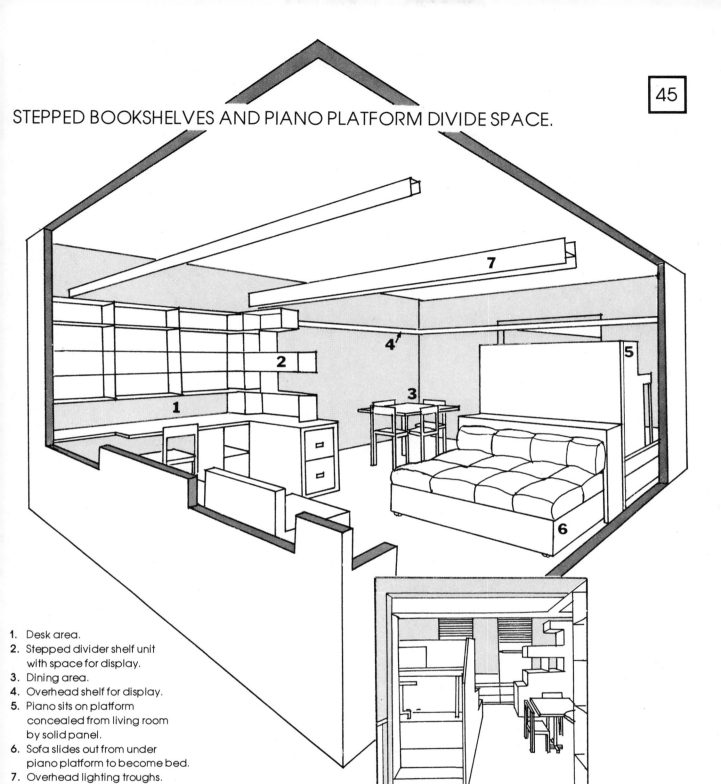

1. Desk area.
2. Stepped divider shelf unit with space for display.
3. Dining area.
4. Overhead shelf for display.
5. Piano sits on platform concealed from living room by solid panel.
6. Sofa slides out from under piano platform to become bed.
7. Overhead lighting troughs.

FROM THE ENTRANCE, BEDROOM/LIVING ROOM AND DESK AREA ARE CONCEALED.

SHARING A SPACE

□

Many clients share a space with someone else. This can range from sharing a room in an apartment as a work space to a marriage to a complex arrangement of several adults sharing an apartment out of mutual friendship or economic convenience.

Sharing an apartment can require unusual solutions. One case involved three roommates who were sharing an apartment. Two loved their cats, but the third was allergic and didn't want them in the kitchen. However, one cat owner's room was accessible only by walking through the kitchen. We designed a combination bench and cat duct—a tube of clear plexiglass through which the cats could move, isolated from the kitchen but still able to reach their room and observe the goings-on. A built-in bench above the tube made the area useful to humans also. Whatever the specific problem, the designs are the products of cooperation and compromise among the people sharing the space.

We designed a study/work area for ten people in a room 16 feet by 20 feet. These clients all did different kinds of research, writing, and teaching involving the use of books, files, and typewriters. After much discussion, eventually everyone figured out what was needed nearby—how high each individual desk should be, what kind of storage space for supplies was needed, what part of the room each person wanted to be in, and the like. At this point we could design the space for them in detail. The time invested in these preliminary discussions paid off in enabling us to design the most efficient use of the space and in savings on costly changes in construction.

The impetus behind these projects usually is the desire for people to get along with each other better. If the space does not work, it can create friction on a personal level. By figuring out a way to make the space work, we make it easier for people to get along.

Marjorie and Harold needed storage space in their new apartment to accommodate all the possessions and clothing accumulated in twenty years of living in a house. Larry and Michael liked working together and wanted a room where they could do so comfortably and efficiently. Jenny and Gordon wanted an elegant loft bedroom in their living room since they had turned the bedroom into an office once they both started working at home. If one roommate sleeps on a convertible couch in the living room and the others have private rooms, everyone will be happier when each has an equal degree of privacy. These are examples of how, when people choose to share a space, they can make the venture work better by designing the space to fit their specific needs and purposes.

15. Couple includes mini-living room and home offices in bedroom

Leslie and Jim both spend busy days at work. In addition they are raising three children, so they wanted to turn their bedroom into a place for retreat, quiet, and writing. They live on the two lower floors of a brownstone with their bedroom located at street level. Leslie is a teacher and is currently writing a book. Jim is in advertising and frequently works on ad copy at home in addition to doing the family finances. Although they both needed desk space, the main priority was to have a sitting area in front of the fireplace and to have the bed feel like a private, separate area. They wanted the room to look modern, clean, and airy. Solution: A two-level central desk structure creates a sitting area in front of the fireplace and a private alcove for the bed. The line of the upper desk is continued around the room and unifies the room's various elements.

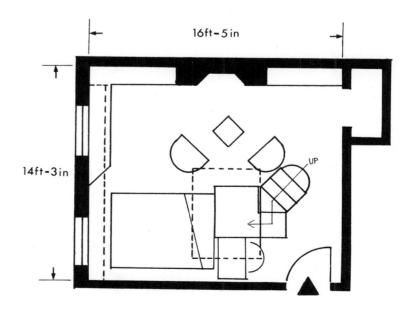

FROM ONE SIDE, A LIVING ROOM AND BEDROOM.

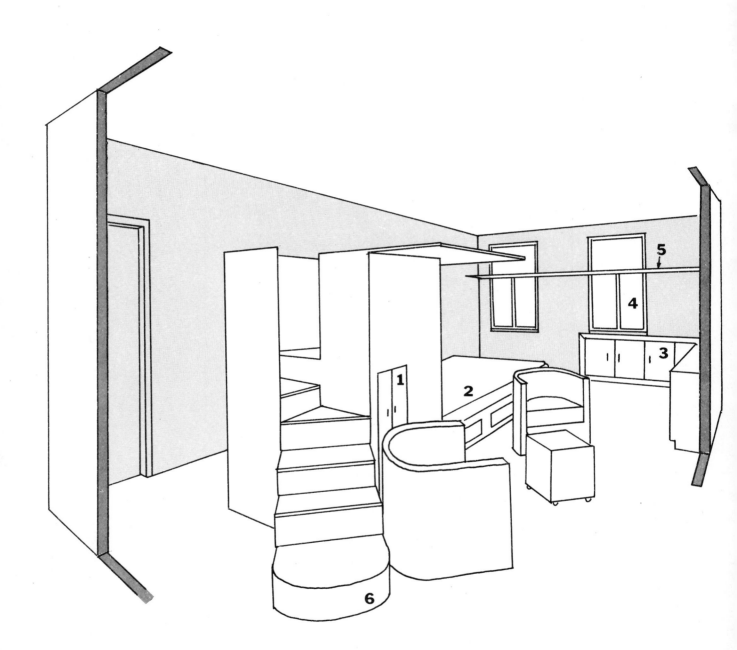

1. Storage space.
2. Bed with drawers.
3. Cabinets.
4. Translucent screens on lower half of windows.
5. Overhead shelf for plants and display.

FROM THE OTHER SIDE, A HOME OFFICE; STAIRS LEAD TO SECOND OFFICE.

51

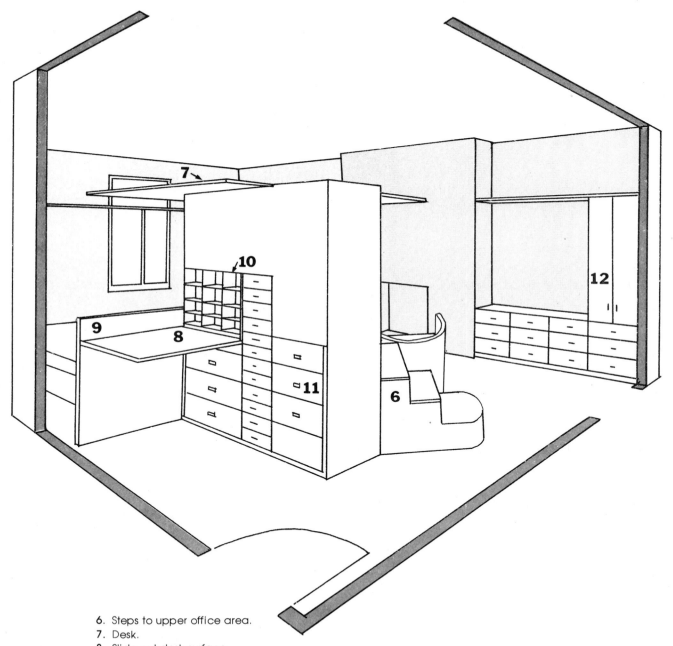

6. Steps to upper office area.
7. Desk.
8. Slide-out desk surface.
9. Bed headboard.
10. Cubbies for papers.
11. File drawers.
12. Clothing unit.

Don and Jo rent a four-room duplex apartment on the ground floor and cellar of a brownstone. For six years they thought they were going to move so they let the cellar go to waste because of the low ceilings, lack of light, and damp walls. When Don started working full-time at home on his writing and apartment prices became prohibitive, they decided to stay, to create an office/guest room upstairs, and to move their bedroom downstairs. Since they had guests almost every weekend during the summer, they liked the idea of the increased comfort and privacy that a downstairs bedroom would give. Solution: The design turns the cellar into a luxury suite with a bedroom and a comfortable sitting/television area. A diagonal closet and closets with shelves under the stairs increase storage. There is also room for displaying Don's miniature-theater and handmade puppet collection. The shelves have a cabinet that holds the kitty litter and has a "private" entrance in back for the cats—another important detail of the design.

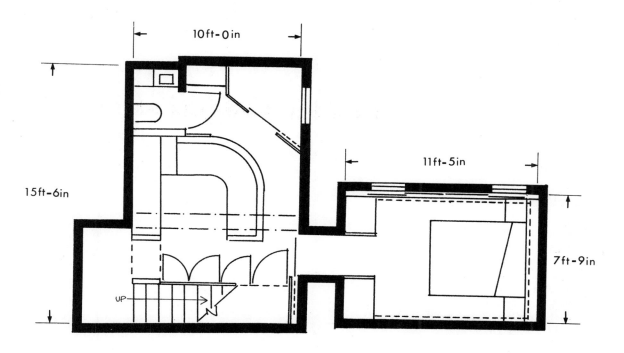

DIAGONAL CLOSET AND CURVED SOFAS CENTER AROUND DISPLAY SHELVES.

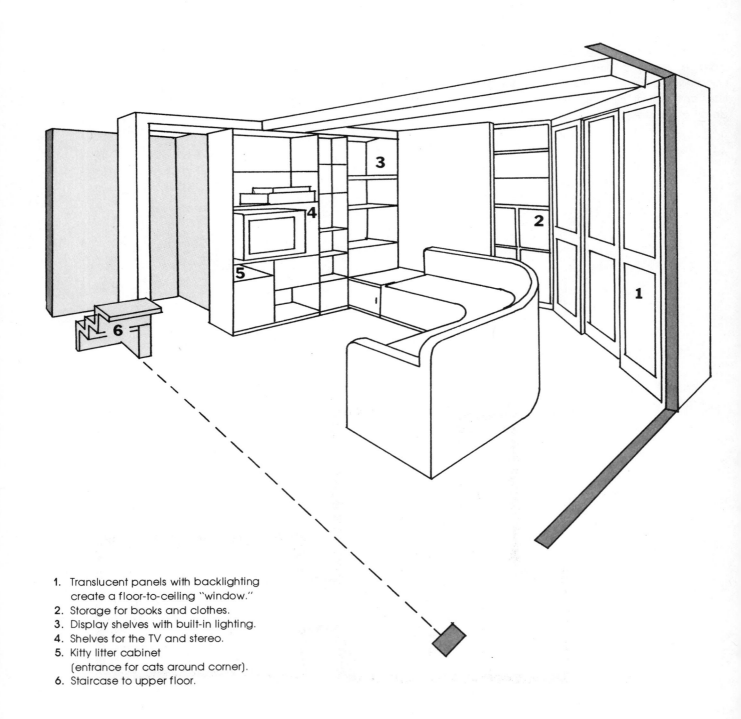

1. Translucent panels with backlighting create a floor-to-ceiling "window."
2. Storage for books and clothes.
3. Display shelves with built-in lighting.
4. Shelves for the TV and stereo.
5. Kitty litter cabinet (entrance for cats around corner).
6. Staircase to upper floor.

SITTING AREA AND SHELF UNIT.

OVERHEAD FRAMES AND HEADBOARD CREATE AN INTIMATE SPACE.

1. Headboard.
2. Sliding panels conceal
   basement window and radiators.
3. Drawers.
4. Dehumidifier cabinet.
5. Lighting troughs.

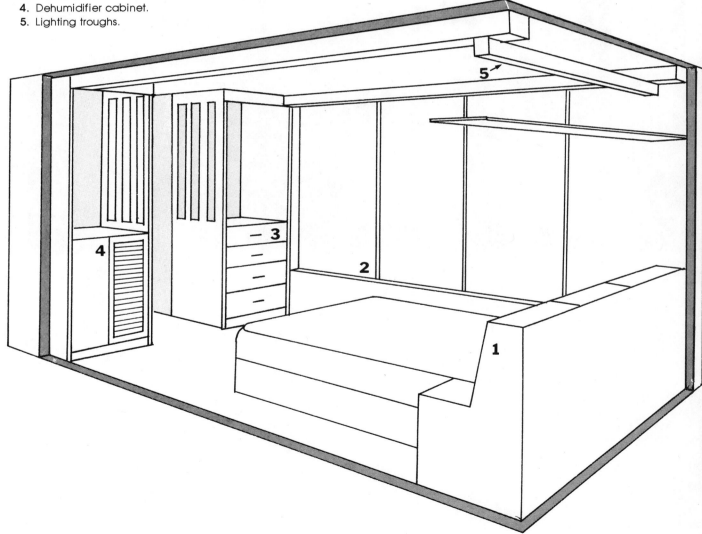

VIEW FROM SITTING AREA INTO BEDROOM.

17. Three roommates get a third bedroom out of a living-room corner

Kim, Jennifer, and Carrie shared a two-bedroom apartment with a large living room. They had been unable to find a three-bedroom apartment to fit their budgets, so they had settled for two large bedrooms with lots of light. Jennifer and Carrie each had one of the bedrooms, and Kim had been sleeping in the living room. Having friends over for parties and casual impromptu dinners was hard on Kim, a nurse, who worked the night shift and also needed to study. She needed room for a double bed, a desk, bookshelves, and a closet. They wanted to see if they could have a dining room and living room and still give Kim the space and privacy she needed. Solution: Bookshelves, closet, and headboard unit all do double duty to separate bedroom and shape the space into living-room and dining-room areas.

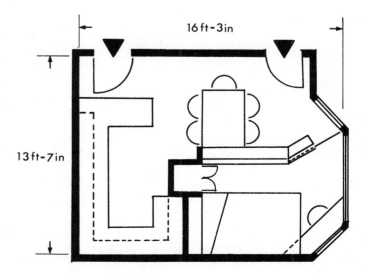

THE ROOM HAS BUILT-IN SEATING AND A SEPARATE DINING AREA.

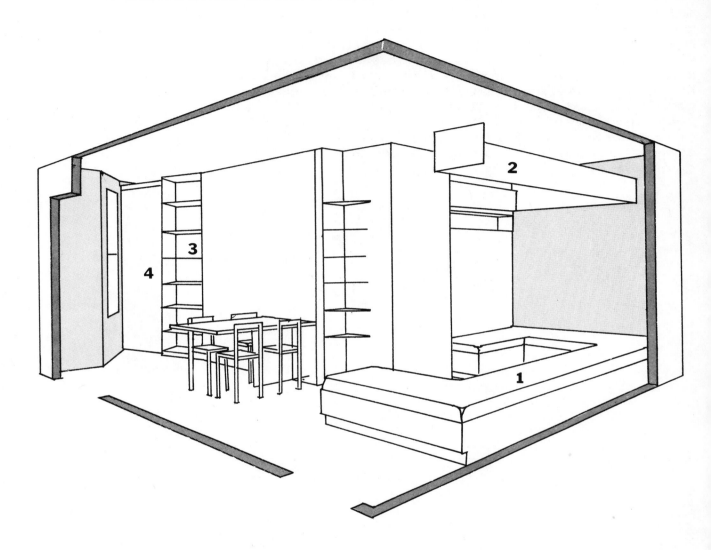

1. Built-in seating, fronts open for storage.
2. Overhead frame defines living room.
3. Bookshelves for shared use.
4. Sliding door to bedroom.

BEDROOM SEPARATED BY SHELF/STORAGE UNIT, CLOSET, AND HEADBOARD UNIT.

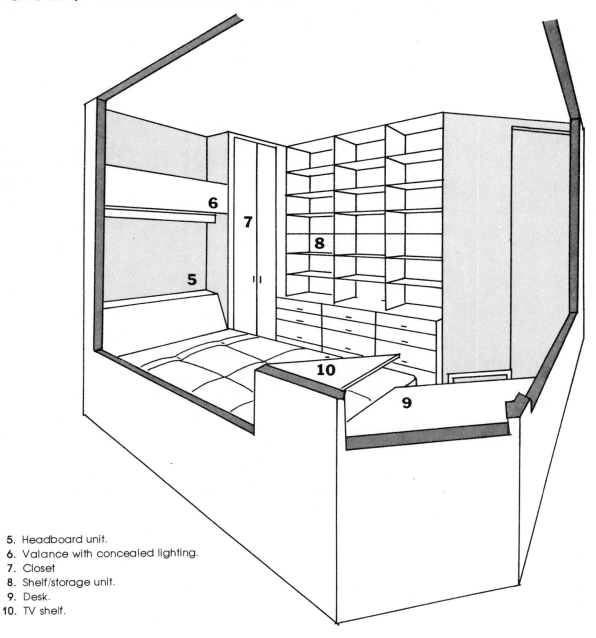

5. Headboard unit.
6. Valance with concealed lighting.
7. Closet
8. Shelf/storage unit.
9. Desk.
10. TV shelf.

18. Painting studio at home for businesswoman with three children

Mara wanted to set up a place to paint in the living room of her apartment. She had started painting several months earlier at her friend's apartment and found that it was a much-needed release from her high-pressure job on Wall Street. Now she wanted a studio in her own apartment so that she could paint more often. She wanted it to be near the windows and to provide complete privacy while she was painting, yet she didn't want to block the view or light from the rest of the room. The studio needed to be compact, since her family used the living room quite often. She also had a small office setup and occasionally had clients over for financial consultations, so she needed to be able to close the studio off from her desk when she was working. Solution: The studio is divided from the living room by a freestanding unit that holds the stereo, cassette player, records, and tapes on the living-room side and has room for painting supplies on the studio side. Levolor blinds and rolling shoji screens can provide Mara with whatever degree of privacy she needs without blocking the light from the living room. The living-room side of the unit is painted the color of the room, and the studio side is polyurethaned to create a different atmosphere. The rest of the studio is made up of a large rolling easel and three units that take up very little floor and wall space when not in use:

(1) An easel mounted on the wall, which can be adjusted to different heights, different angles, and can expand for larger paintings. The easel slides across the wall so that it can be stored out of the way or be easily pulled out for painting.

(2) A bookcase that holds books and supplies in its upper section and has a fold-up drawing/desk surface in its lower section. The surface is stored flat against the back of the bookcase and can be folded up and adjusted to any angle desired for drawing or writing.

(3) A cart with drawers and shelves for supplies. The drawers can be pulled all the way out and become separate boxes for carrying and organizing tubes of paint. The top of the cart has a recessed section for holding jars of paint and liquids. The cart is on wheels and can be rolled into any position convenient to either the easel or the drawing table.

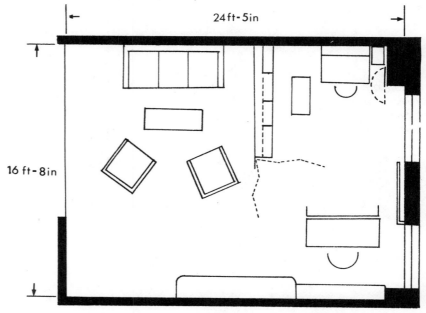

24 ft - 5 in

16 ft - 8 in

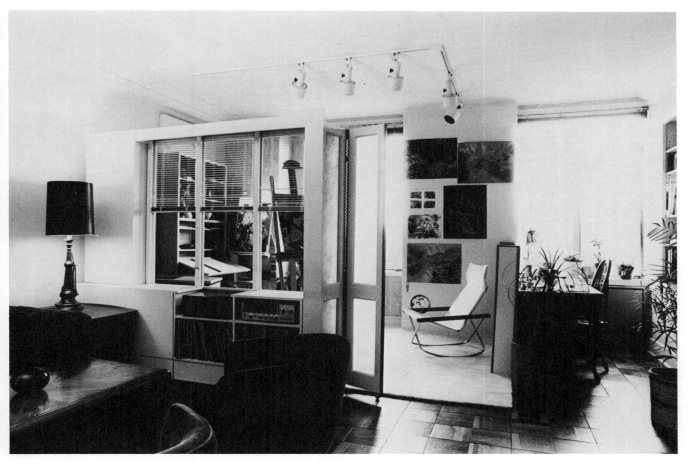

DIVIDER SEPARATES ART STUDIO FROM LIVING ROOM.

CART, FOLD-UP DESK IN BOOKCASE,
AND SLIDING EASEL ORGANIZE INTERIOR OF STUDIO.

ON THE OTHER SIDE, DIVIDER HOLDS SUPPLIES.

19. Corner of living room becomes computer office for financial planner

Daniel and Patricia had just bought their apartment and wanted to do it over to meet their needs. Daniel, a financial planner, and Patricia, a fashion designer and gourmet cook, each needed specific elements incorporated into the design. We designed additional clothes storage and a dressing area for Patricia and redesigned what had been a tiny galley kitchen into a kitchen with full-size appliances and space for Patricia to work. This left the corner of the living room as a computer study for Daniel. Daniel needed to be separated from the living room in order to work, but he didn't want to feel closed in or to make the living room feel smaller. He needed a lot of bookshelves for his reference materials and a place for the computer keyboard, monitor, and printer but still wanted a large desk surface. He also needed space for his files and computer discs. Solution: Daniel's study is a U-shaped arrangement built of oak plywood in the corner of the living room. The dividing unit holds the television and stereo equipment on the living-room side and Daniel's slide-out keyboard, discs, and lateral filing cabinet on the study side. It is stepped in three stages to provide privacy for Daniel yet not overpower the living room.

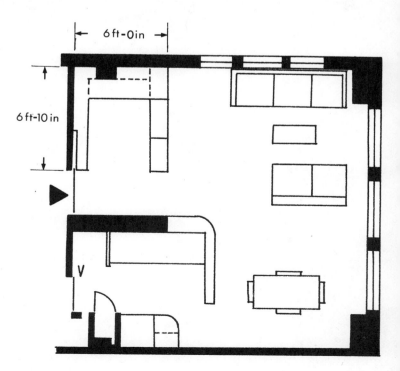

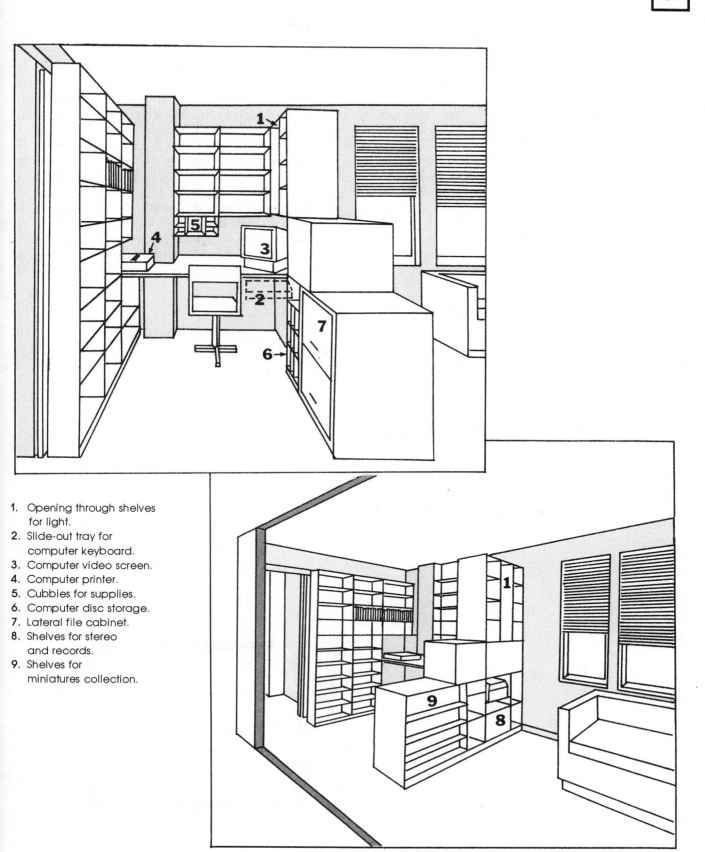

1. Opening through shelves for light.
2. Slide-out tray for computer keyboard.
3. Computer video screen.
4. Computer printer.
5. Cubbies for supplies.
6. Computer disc storage.
7. Lateral file cabinet.
8. Shelves for stereo and records.
9. Shelves for miniatures collection.

20. Writer and composer fix up
a study to share

Michael had just moved into a two-bedroom apartment and was looking forward to setting up a study in one of the rooms where he and his friend, Larry, could work. Michael is a composer, and Larry writes screenplays for movies. They had been friends since college, had collaborated on several projects, and liked working together. They wanted to set up a space where each could have everything he needed within easy reach and enough room to spread out without getting in the other's way. Michael liked to work on a large slanted desk surface with a lot of additional desk surface around him. He also needed a place near his work surface to store the large sheets of paper that were works in progress. Larry needed plenty of bookshelf space for his extensive library, several filing cabinets, and a place for his typewriter. They both worked long hours and wanted the room to feel comfortable and conducive to work. Solution: Desk surface and bookshelves wrap around the room. A large central surface is the main work area.

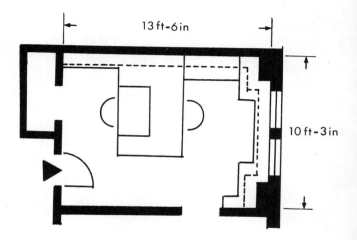

WRAPAROUND DESK AND SHELVES PROVIDE SPACE FOR WRITING AND COMPOSING.

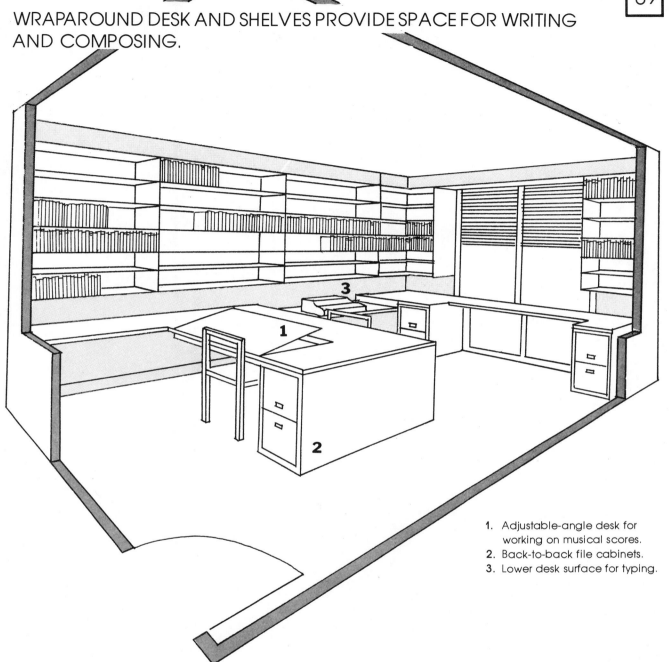

1. Adjustable-angle desk for working on musical scores.
2. Back-to-back file cabinets.
3. Lower desk surface for typing.

FAMILIES

☐

Some of our clients are parents raising children. Often the family situations are complex, involving children from previous marriages. Sometimes children just stay over on occasional weekends, and sometimes a new household has formed. Several times we have planned for a child who was still months from being born. The parents usually have several interests, such as art or a home business, in addition to their family and their full-time jobs. All these activities need to be planned for. The most common reason for making changes in a couple's apartment is a new child. The child needs to be provided for. The changes that need to be made can't be put off and can't be avoided. Most people would rather not incur the expense of a complete move to a bigger place at the same time that they are having a child, so the problem becomes how to provide space in the existing apartment.

In most homes, the largest room is the living room. The pressure for space leads to some uncommon solutions for these often underused spaces. This can be the inclusion of a bedroom for parents or children or a studio or a home office.

Families are a unit, but they are made up of individuals with specific personal needs. Ruth Ann wanted a place to display her pottery; Maxine needed a place to conduct makeup classes; and Jack needed a place for his Buddhist temple where he could chant in privacy. In addition to their often quite small rooms, the children always need space to play in. Each of these individual needs must be included in the designs.

21. Living room remodeled to include parents' bedroom

Jane and Richard were expecting their second child, and with it they were also expecting a space crunch in their one-bedroom brownstone apartment. They did not want to move since they loved the location—less than a block from Central Park and only a few blocks from their son's school. In addition, the apartment had a spectacular living room with a large, curved bay window, 14-foot-high ceilings, and elaborate architectural details such as an ornate marble fireplace. They wanted to give the children the bedroom and to make a bedroom for themselves in the living room. The answer was clearly to design a second level in the living room, but this would have to be done in a way that would give them privacy while preserving both the physical and aesthetic integrity of the space. The new construction also needed to harmonize with their antique furniture. Solution: The new bedroom is incorporated into a loft structure that becomes part of the architecture by giving a new sense of volume and interest to the room. The structure has separate areas for the bed, clothes storage, and dressing, and even an area for the baby's crib that can later be made into an additional closet. The entire structure can be assembled and taken apart with a screwdriver and a wrench.

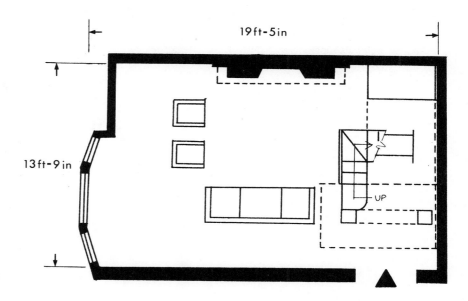

SECOND LEVEL IN LIVING ROOM MAKES NEW BEDROOM.

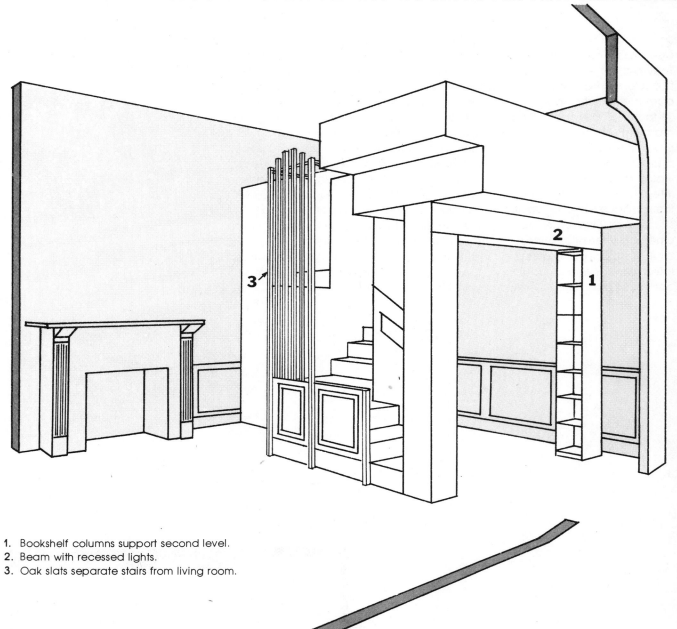

1. Bookshelf columns support second level.
2. Beam with recessed lights.
3. Oak slats separate stairs from living room.

VIEW FROM ABOVE SHOWS BED AND CRIB AREA.

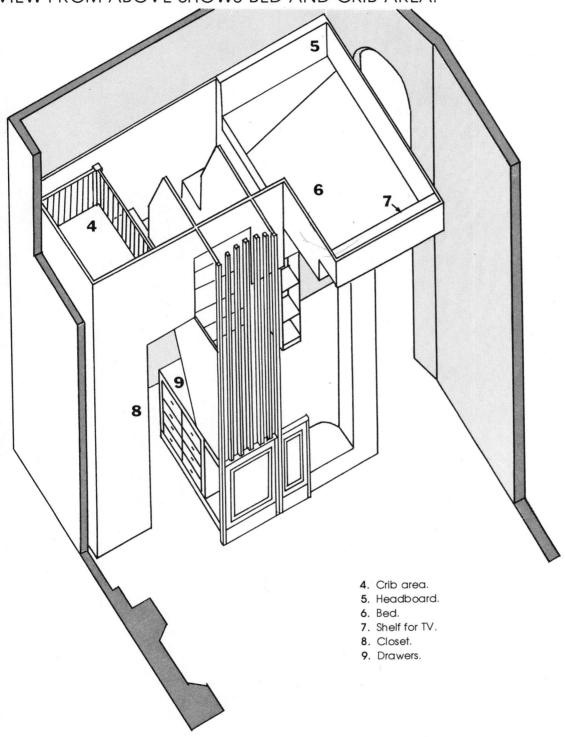

4. Crib area.
5. Headboard.
6. Bed.
7. Shelf for TV.
8. Closet.
9. Drawers.

Maxine and Paul were excitedly expecting the birth of their first child and wanted to make a room for the baby. The only space available in their one-bedroom apartment was in the living room, so some kind of divider was required. But this was only the beginning of what they needed. Two children from Paul's previous marriage needed a place to stay over on occasional weekends. Maxine teaches skin care and sells cosmetics, and Paul has a private financial-planning concern; both businesses operate out of the home. They also wanted a living-room area with sofas, a dining room to seat eight, and a stereo center. A further complication was that the room had an unusual shape, a condition typical of buildings in their neighborhood. Solution: The design concept allows for flexibility in the degree of separation between areas—between the living room and dining room and especially between the living room and the baby's room. In addition, each area functions in several ways. A "wall of boxes" allows for flexible control of light, sound, and air between the baby's room and the living room. Stereo speakers and display shelves are built into this wall. A "tower" and lighting bridge separate the dining room from the living room and are oriented to work with the angled wall.

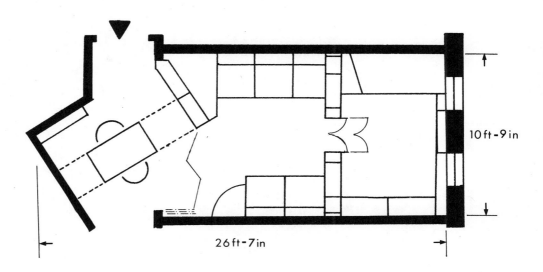

10 ft - 9 in

26 ft - 7 in

SPACE IS DIVIDED BY DISPLAY WALL AND TOWER.

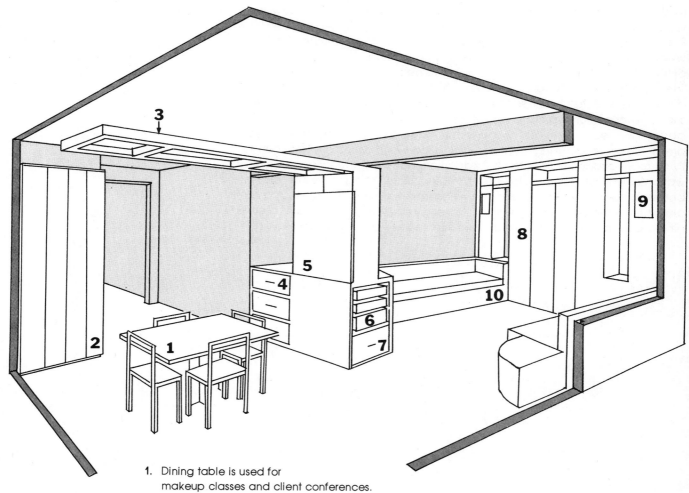

1. Dining table is used for makeup classes and client conferences.
2. Storage cabinet for dining room chairs.
3. Overhead lighting frame defines dining area; provides different light for eating and makeup classes.
4. File drawers.
5. Shelf unit for makeup inventory.
6. Stereo components on slide-out shelves.
7. Drawer for records.
8. Wall with display windows separates baby's room from living room.
9. Stereo speakers built into wall.
10. Sofa bed for visiting child.

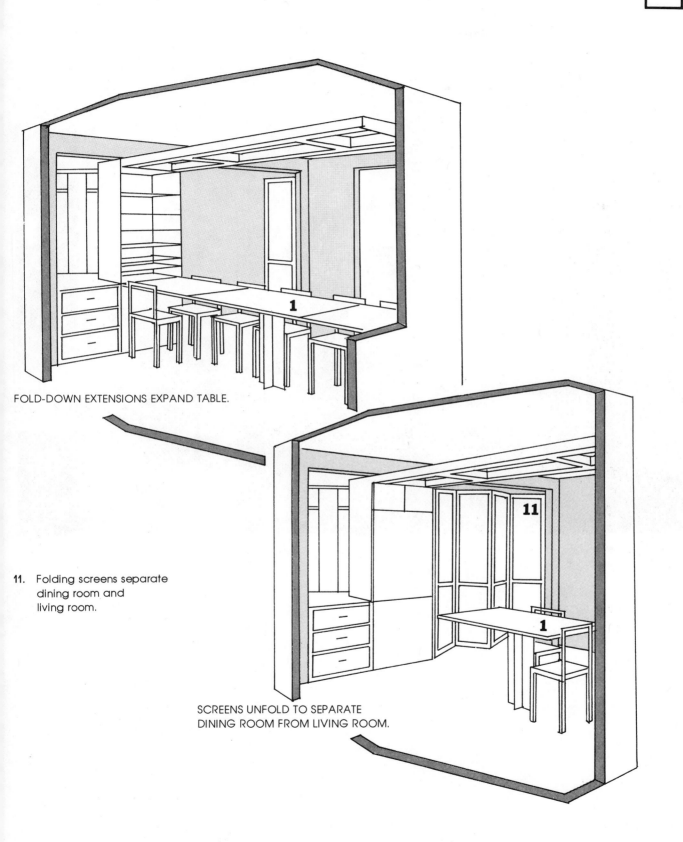

FOLD-DOWN EXTENSIONS EXPAND TABLE.

11. Folding screens separate
dining room and
living room.

SCREENS UNFOLD TO SEPARATE
DINING ROOM FROM LIVING ROOM.

VIEW FROM LIVING ROOM
INTO THE DINING AREA.

TABLE WITH EXTENSIONS FOLDED DOWN.

DIVIDING SCREEN PARTLY CLOSED.

THREE ARRANGEMENTS OF THE CHILD'S ROOM.

FOR OLDER CHILD.

FOR BABY.

FOR SLEEPOVER GUEST.

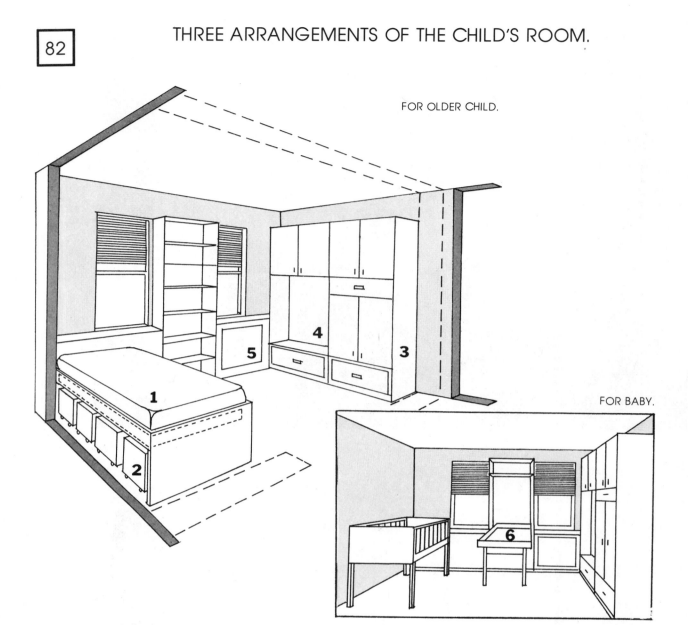

1. Bed (installed when child is old enough).
2. Rolling boxes.
3. Cabinets for clothing and toys.
4. Blackboard panel conceals fold-out bed.
5. Radiator cover.
6. Removable fold-down changing table.
7. Fold-out bed rests on rolling boxes.
8. Mattress for fold-out bed.
9. Shelves (substituted for changing table).

OVERHEAD VIEW SHOWS DIVISION OF SPACE.

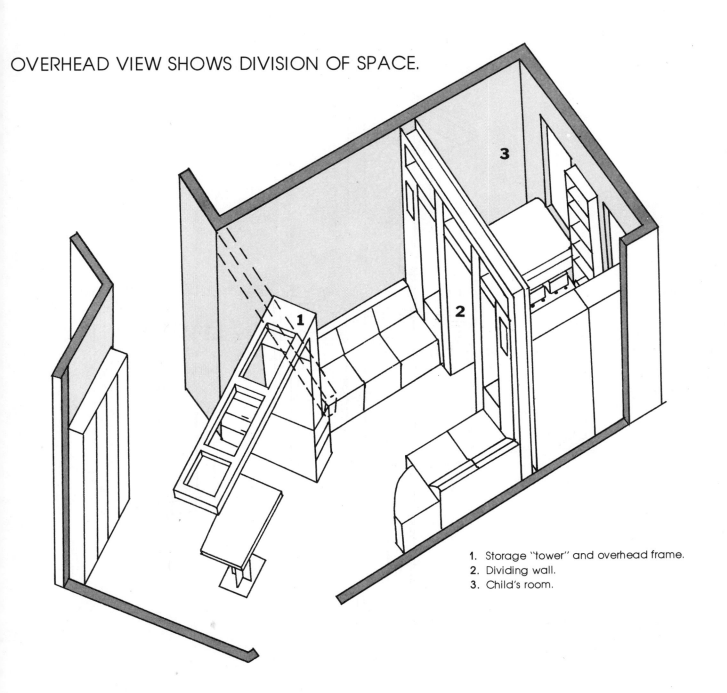

1. Storage "tower" and overhead frame.
2. Dividing wall.
3. Child's room.

DIVIDING WALL MADE UP OF SEPARATE BOXES.

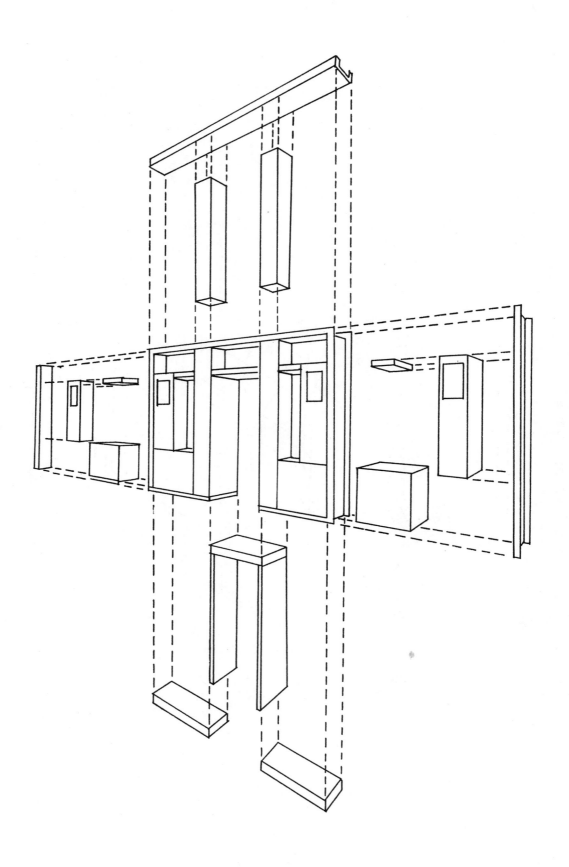

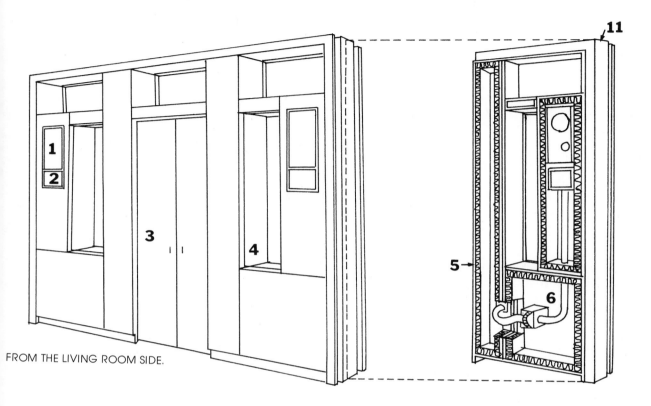

FROM THE LIVING ROOM SIDE.

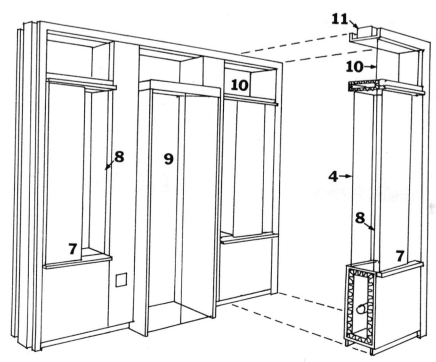

1. Built-in speakers.
2. Ventilation grilles.
3. Solid doors for soundproofing.
4. Hinged plexiglass for access to display shelves.
5. Fiberglass insulation for noise control.
6. Ventilation fan and duct.
7. Sliding wood panels to block light from living room.
8. Fixed plexiglass for soundproofing living room.
9. Three-eighths-inch-thick plexiglass doors block sound but allow light from outside windows into living room.
10. Fixed plexiglass panels on overhead display shelves.
11. Foam rubber strip seals edges of wall.

FROM THE BEDROOM SIDE.

Ruth Ann and Jerry were desperate. The main room in their small three-room apartment (which had to serve as kitchen, dining room, and living room for themselves, their seven-year-old daughter Megan, and their dog Emily) had been cramped enough when their daughter was born but now it had become worse. They had tried various pieces of furniture, including three different couches, and had installed full-length mirrors along one wall, but nothing made the room function better or look bigger. There was no place to watch television comfortably; the dining-room table was always in the way; and the kitchen was so small that it was impossible to work in. Ruth Ann did not have enough counter space to prepare meals; she had a sink that was not large enough to wash pots and barely enough room for a jar of peanut butter and a loaf of bread in her under-the-counter refrigerator. She couldn't cook anything ahead of time because her freezer was only big enough for an ice-cube tray. They found that they avoided having company over because there was no room, and they felt embarrassed by their home. Ruth Ann found the room depressing, especially in the evening while Jerry was at work and she was at home after Megan had gone to sleep. They wanted help and they wanted it fast. Solution: A tower located off-center in the room, away from the entrance, separates the kitchen from the rest of the room, houses the large refrigerator-freezer, and has space for storage. The kitchen has a full-size sink, dishwasher, stove, and oven. It can be entered from either side of the tower, which eliminates traffic jams. Full-length sliding translucent screens, with lights behind them, conceal windows overlooking a sunless courtyard. The mirrors now reflect the room and the screens giving depth to the space and making the room look larger.

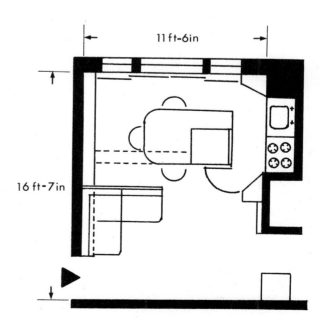

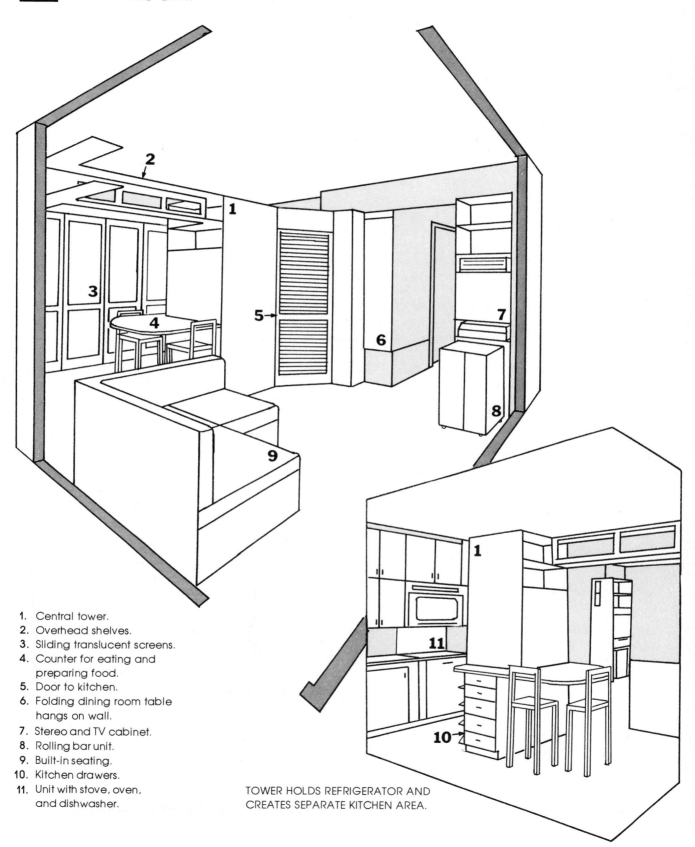

1. Central tower.
2. Overhead shelves.
3. Sliding translucent screens.
4. Counter for eating and preparing food.
5. Door to kitchen.
6. Folding dining room table hangs on wall.
7. Stereo and TV cabinet.
8. Rolling bar unit.
9. Built-in seating.
10. Kitchen drawers.
11. Unit with stove, oven, and dishwasher.

TOWER HOLDS REFRIGERATOR AND CREATES SEPARATE KITCHEN AREA.

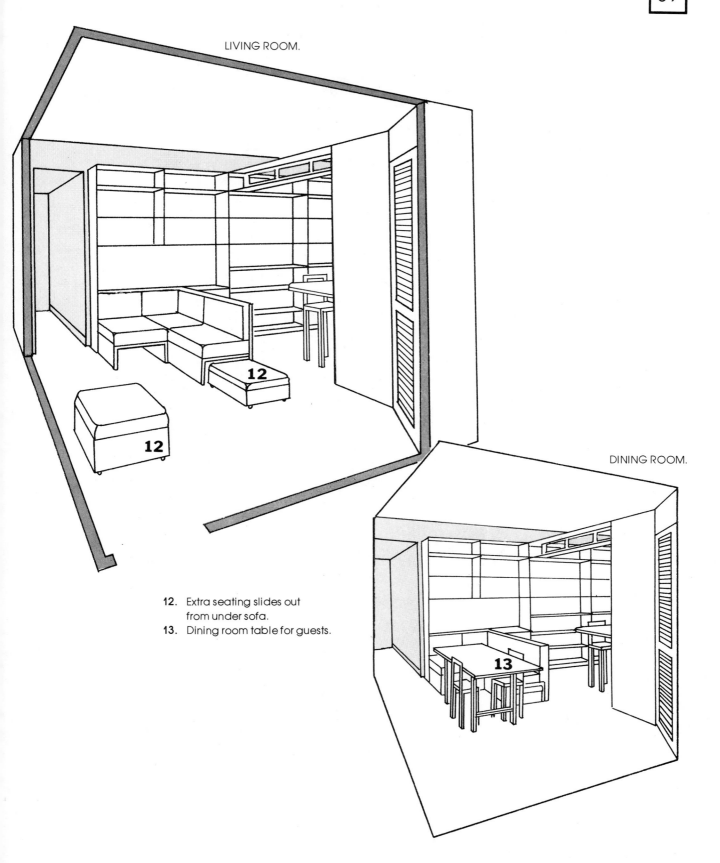

LIVING ROOM.

DINING ROOM.

12. Extra seating slides out
from under sofa.
13. Dining room table for guests.

NEW CONSTRUCTION SEPARATES ROOM INTO THREE AREAS.

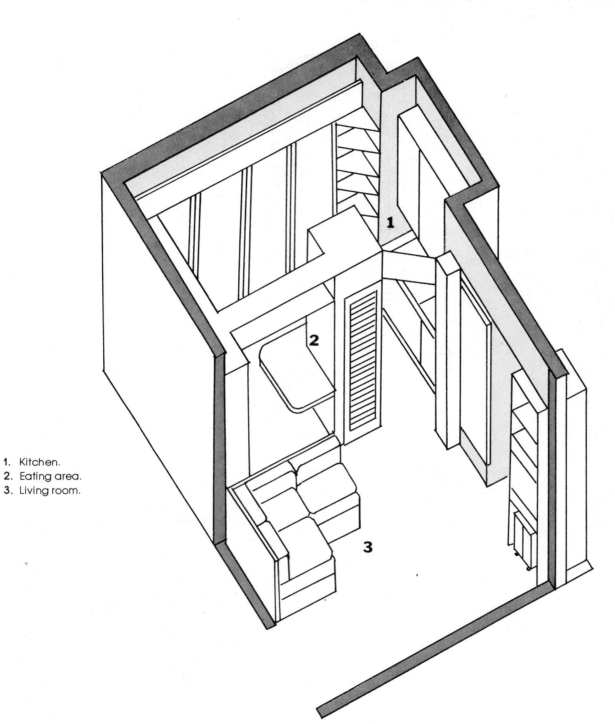

1. Kitchen.
2. Eating area.
3. Living room.

TV AND STEREO CABINET.

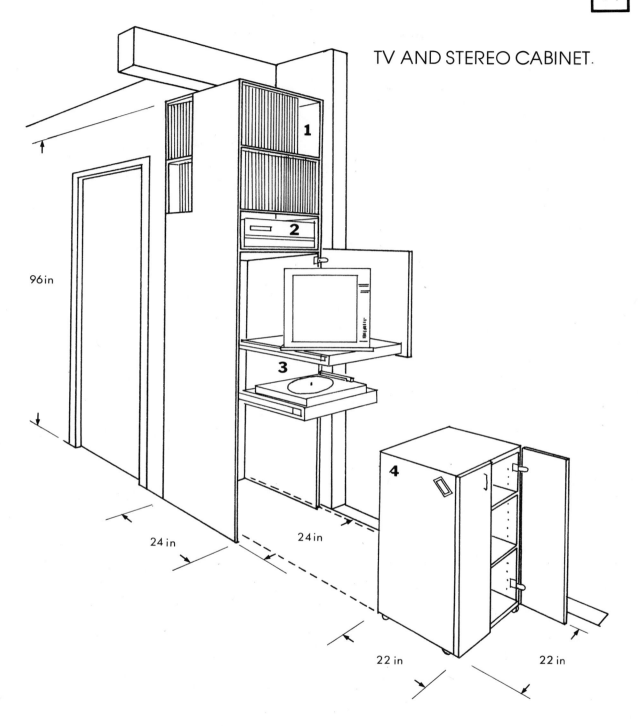

96 in

24 in

24 in

22 in

22 in

1. Record shelves.
2. Amplifier.
3. Slide-out shelves for TV and turntable.
4. Bar cart with adjustable shelves.

CHILDREN

□

When a child's room gets fixed up, it becomes a special event in the child's life. He or she usually becomes involved in the process, strikes up a relationship with the carpenter and painter, and checks on the progress of the job with many questions. When three-year-old Pamela's "tree house" structure was being built, she and Wayne, the carpenter, became friends. Wayne showed her how to use a screwdriver and hammer and even taught her how to dance to some of her records. Later, when a repair was needed, Pamela stuck close by, watching every move. She then proceeded to pick up the screwdriver and work on the broken hinge herself. In connection with another project, a four-year-old boy proudly keeps a picture of himself and the carpenter standing in his newly completed room.

Of course, in the process many parents secretly wish to have a room like their child's. During the construction of a room for his eight-year-old daughter, one father kept a careful eye on every detail. When the ladder to the loft was installed, he expressed grave doubts about the design since he could not climb up the ladder. Only after we had pointed out that it was not really designed for someone his size did he sigh and admit wistfully, "You know, you're right, but I wish I was a kid again. I always wanted something like this." Sometimes children have a chance to try out some of their own ideas about color or certain other aspects of the design. But when their rooms are fixed up, the real importance of the experience is that their special needs have been noticed and have been responded to.

Steven and Nancy moved into a two-bedroom apartment so that their seven-year-old son, Bruce, could have his own room. They got rid of Bruce's old furniture, which was either too young for him or too makeshift and wanted to start all over in Bruce's new room. They wanted the room to have a minimum of furniture so that Bruce and his friends would have plenty of space to play in. Bruce wanted to be able to move his furniture around himself and to incorporate it into his games, so it needed to be lightweight and sturdy. In addition to his bed and storage space for his clothes and games, he needed a surface area for drawing, assembling models, and later for doing homework. Steven had some carpentry experience, so he was planning to build the furniture himself with the help of a friend who was a carpenter. Solution: Rolling shelf units and nesting tables provide plenty of storage space, seating, and surface area. They can be arranged in any manner for different kinds of play. The bed, which was put together out of a few pieces of precut plywood, has a pull-out mattress so that a friend can stay over.

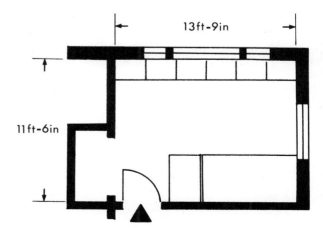

FURNITURE CAN BE MOVED FOR CHANGING ACTIVITIES.

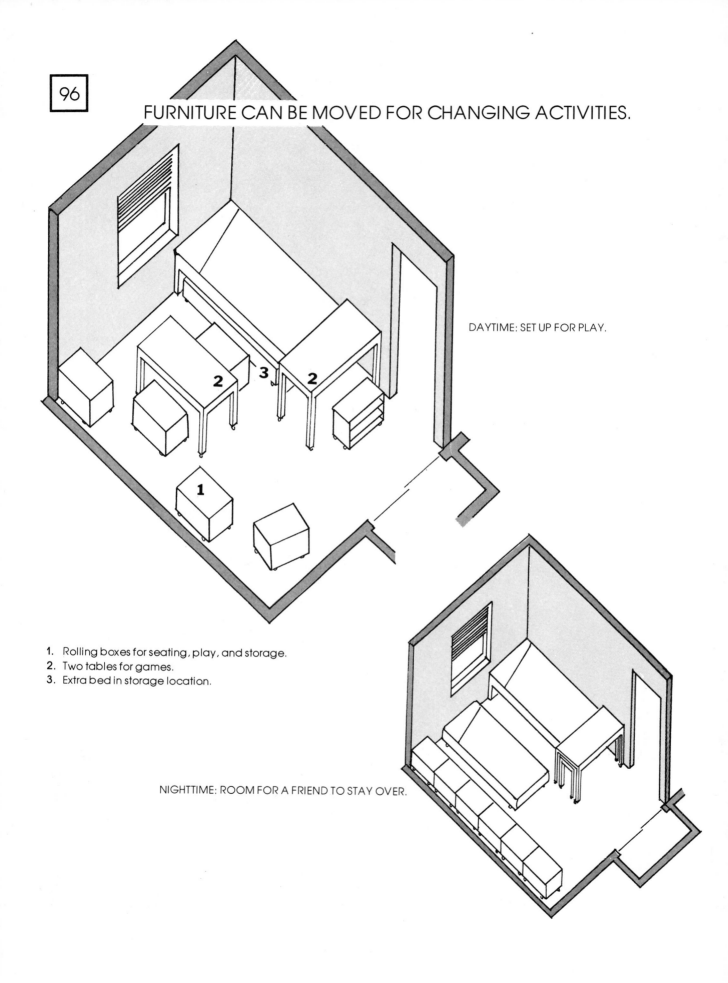

DAYTIME: SET UP FOR PLAY.

1. Rolling boxes for seating, play, and storage.
2. Two tables for games.
3. Extra bed in storage location.

NIGHTTIME: ROOM FOR A FRIEND TO STAY OVER.

THREE BASIC UNITS MAKE UP THE ROOM.

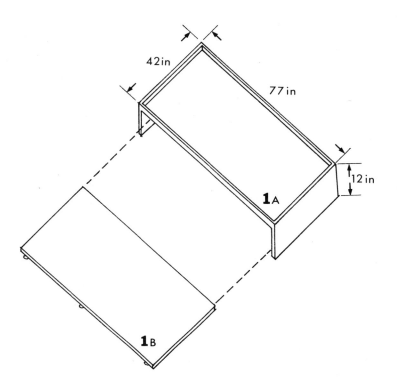

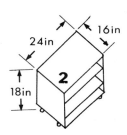

1A. Bed for a single mattress.
1B. Piece of plywood on six swivel wheels
holds the spare mattress.
2. Rolling boxes with
adjustable dividers.
3. Nesting tables.

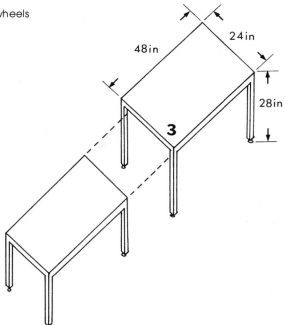

25. Maid's room renovated for an active eight-year-old girl

When Marisa and her two daughters joined forces with Bob and his daughter, there was one major problem. Rachael and Samara both liked their bedrooms, but Jena, Marisa's eight-year-old, ended up with the small maid's room off the kitchen. She didn't have space for all her toys, games, and stuffed animals or room for friends to stay over. She also needed space for a desk, bookshelves, and additional clothing storage. Bob and Marisa were beginning to look for a bigger apartment even though their present apartment was ideal in every other aspect, when they decided to see if something could be done to make Jena's room work and make her feel that it was a special place just for her. Solution: Stacked clothes-storage units, a bed with sliding trundle bed, and drawers, bookshelves, cabinets, and a curved fold-up desk line the walls without overpowering the room. An overhead play-platform/loft bed, which can be removed when Jena outgrows it, spans the width of the room and changes the long and narrow proportions of the room to make it feel larger.

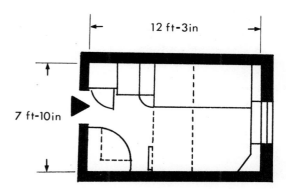

PLAY SPACE AND STORAGE COMBINED IN NEW CONSTRUCTION.

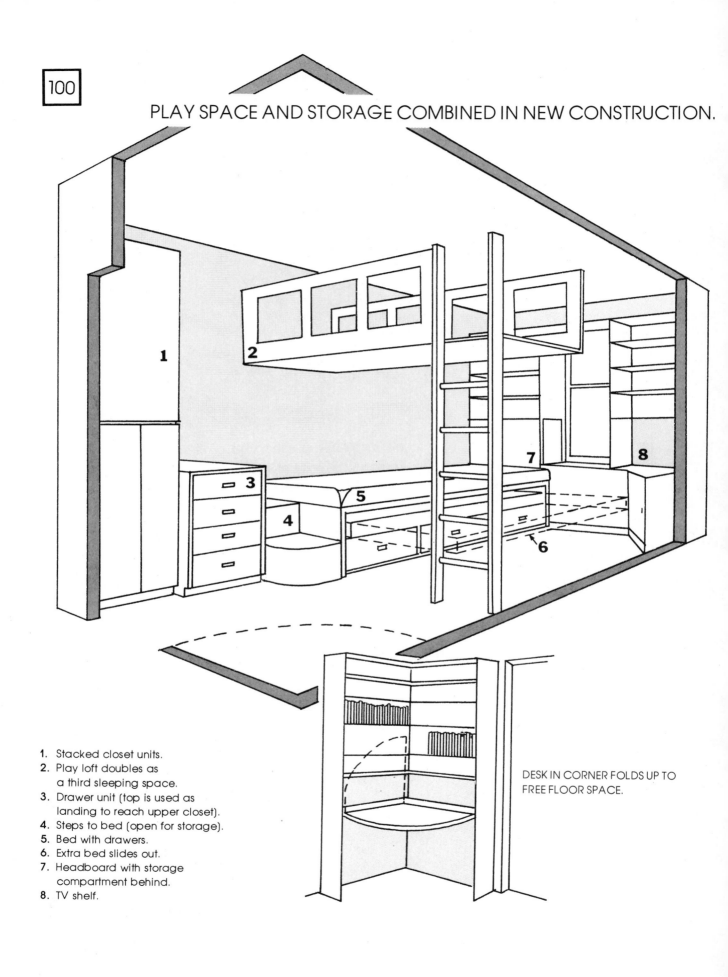

1. Stacked closet units.
2. Play loft doubles as
   a third sleeping space.
3. Drawer unit (top is used as
   landing to reach upper closet).
4. Steps to bed (open for storage).
5. Bed with drawers.
6. Extra bed slides out.
7. Headboard with storage
   compartment behind.
8. TV shelf.

DESK IN CORNER FOLDS UP TO
FREE FLOOR SPACE.

CLOSE-UP OF BED AND STORAGE UNIT.

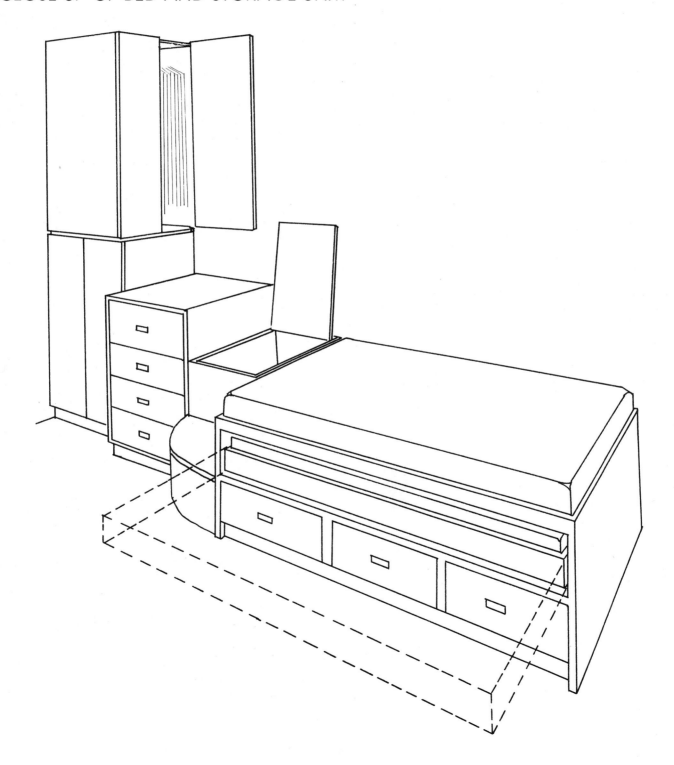

26. Dining alcove becomes a room for a three-year-old

Jon and Jitka's son, Joseph, had just turned three and his bed in the living room of their one-bedroom apartment just wasn't working anymore. His toys and clothes were all over the place, and he hated being displaced to his parent's bedroom when they had company in the evening. He needed a place to play without knocking over his parent's expensive antique furniture. The only place that could be made into a room for Joseph, however, was a dining alcove next to the kitchen that was also the passage between the kitchen and the foyer. The space was just wide enough to accommodate a bed and still allow room to walk through. There wasn't even enough room for a chest of drawers, let alone space for Joseph to play or have any privacy as he got older. Jon and Jitka planned to move within five years, but in the meantime they wanted Joseph to have a room that didn't feel like just a temporary solution. Solution: The room is organized on three platform levels. The bed folds up against the wall in order to increase the available floor space for play and yet give Joseph enough room for his clothes and toys.

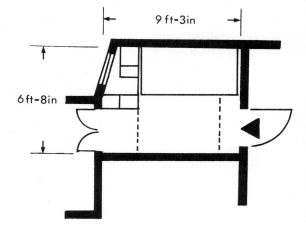

DIFFERENT LEVELS ACCOMMODATE EXTRA PLAY SPACE.

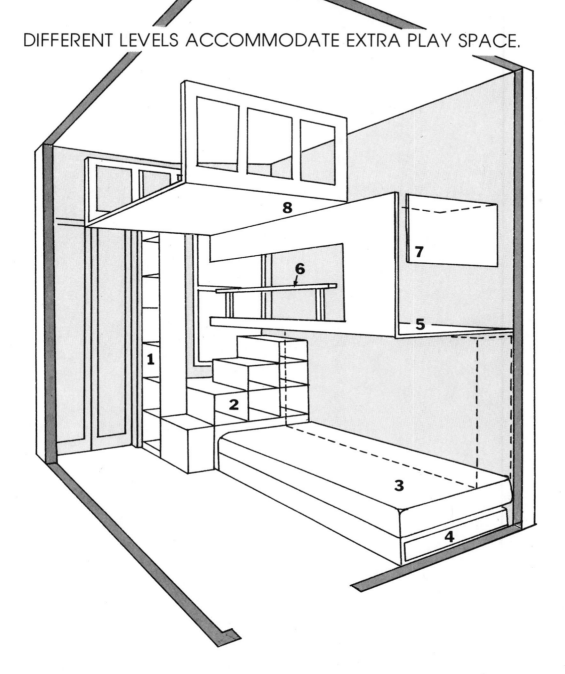

1. Shelves for toys.
2. Steps with storage underneath.
3. Fold-up bed with extra
   mattress stored underneath.
4. Extra mattress.
5. Middle level doubles as play area and
   space for extra mattress.
6. Removable railing.
7. Fold-up desk surface.
8. Upper level for play
   and toy storage.

27. Corner of a living room becomes a room for a thirteen-year-old

Thirteen-year-old Stephanie had a bed and a desk in the dining alcove outside the kitchen in the apartment she lived in with her mother. Stephanie was very unhappy with this situation, as she really needed some privacy. Her desk was piled high with her clothes and books, and her stereo and computer sat useless on top of her mother's piano. She also needed a place where she could hang out with friends without feeling conspicuous and a place where she could keep her cocker spaniel. Solution: Three basic units convert this corner into a room similar to a cabin on a ship, complete with sleeping, storage, and desk space. There is even room to have a friend stay overnight.

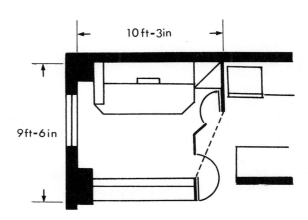

SHELF UNIT SEPARATES BEDROOM FROM LIVING ROOM.

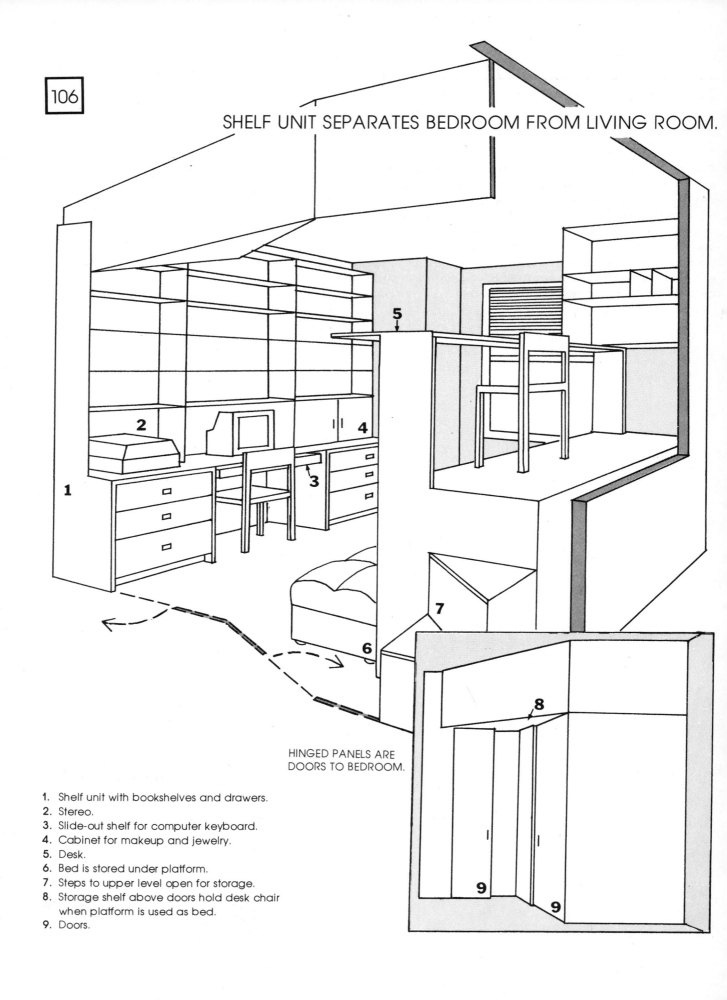

HINGED PANELS ARE
DOORS TO BEDROOM.

1. Shelf unit with bookshelves and drawers.
2. Stereo.
3. Slide-out shelf for computer keyboard.
4. Cabinet for makeup and jewelry.
5. Desk.
6. Bed is stored under platform.
7. Steps to upper level open for storage.
8. Storage shelf above doors hold desk chair
   when platform is used as bed.
9. Doors.

14

5

13

12

11

10

10. Bed rolled out for sleeping.
11. Compartment for extra mattress.
12. Bed rolled out partway for seating.
13. Storage compartment.
14. Shelves for schoolwork.

DESK PLATFORM DOUBLES AS EXTRA SLEEPING SPACE.

Rita and Jesse were in the process of redoing their entire apartment, including the room of their active nine-year-old son, Eric. None of the furniture that they had looked at left enough room for Eric's athletic equipment or for him to build models or for a friend to stay over. They had considered a loft bed but didn't like the idea of Eric using a ladder at night. Besides, a loft bed still didn't leave them with space to put Eric's clothes, stereo, and desk without taking up all the floor space. Solution: A "trundle loft bed" with steps instead of a ladder conserves floor space. The steps provide storage for clothes, stereo, books, records, and even nesting tables used for studying and hobbies. A walkway gives access to the beds, which slide across the room for sleeping. A "gantry" holds athletic equipment. A television on a motorized lift can be watched from either bed or floor level.

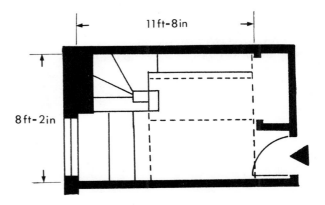

MOVABLE ELEMENTS ALLOW FOR A VARIETY OF ACTIVITIES.

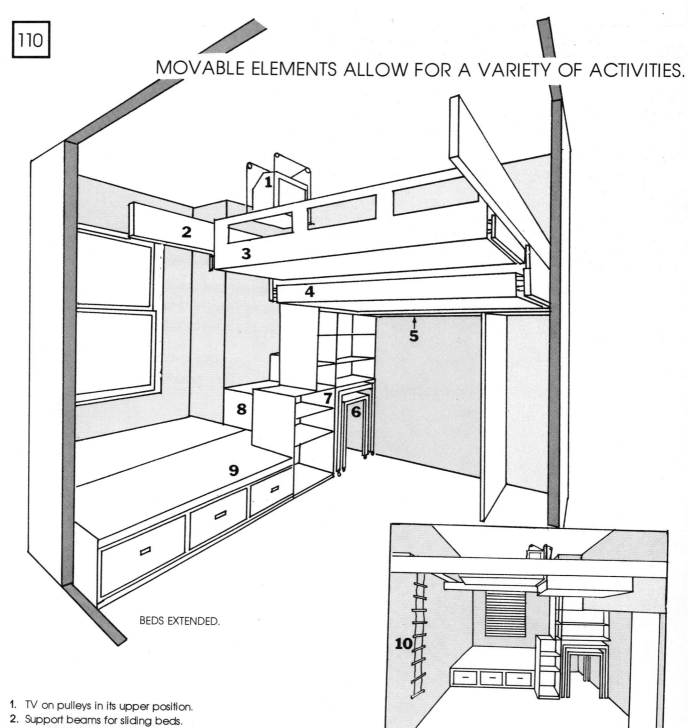

BEDS EXTENDED.

LADDER GANTRY STORED AGAINST WALL.

1. TV on pulleys in its upper position.
2. Support beams for sliding beds.
3. Upper bed, slides toward wall to be stored above lower bed.
4. Lower bed slides toward wall to be stored above walkway.
5. Walkway along wall to reach beds when they are extended out.
6. Nesting tables, stored below steps.
7. Shelves for record player and records.
8. Steps up to beds.
9. Platform with drawers.
10. Ladder gantry.

BEDS IN STORAGE POSITION.

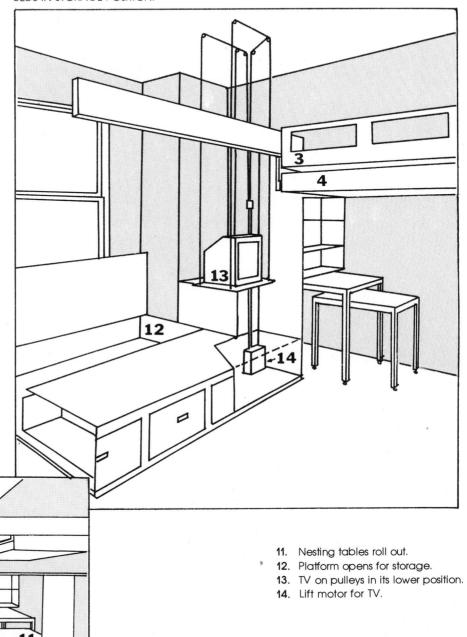

LADDER GANTRY PULLED OUT.

11. Nesting tables roll out.
12. Platform opens for storage.
13. TV on pulleys in its lower position.
14. Lift motor for TV.

Karen and David had bought their two-bedroom duplex apartment in a land-mark building in Soho two years ago. When Karen was six months pregnant with their second child, they wanted to fix up the front room for their two-and-a-half-year-old daughter Pamela and the new baby to share. It was a large, sunny room with its own bathroom and a high ceiling, but there were no closets and the off-center location of the windows made it difficult to divide the room equally. Karen wanted the children to have separate rooms that could accom-modate the children's changing needs as they got older. She wanted the rooms to be fun, exciting places for the children and their friends in addition to having plenty of closet and storage space. While little Pamela and the baby were young, she wanted both beds on floor level, but she thought it would be fun for them to have different levels for sleep and play to expand into later. Solution: A multilevel structure divides the room and provides several sleeping and play areas, as well as desks, shelves, drawers, and closets for both children. When the children are older, doors will be added at both ends and in the staircase for increased separation between the rooms. While the children are young, the whole structure is a big plaything, but later it will provide the privacy and space needed for studying and relaxing.

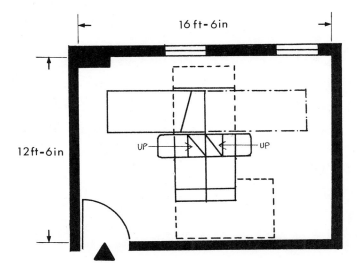

STRUCTURE HAS DIFFERENT LEVELS FOR DIFFERENT ACTIVITIES.

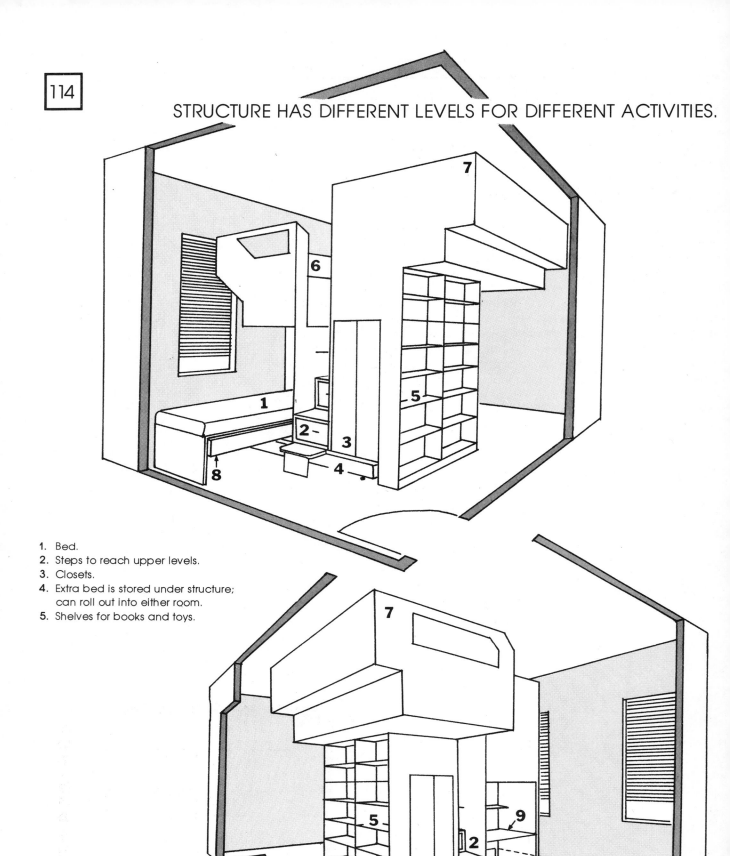

1. Bed.
2. Steps to reach upper levels.
3. Closets.
4. Extra bed is stored under structure; can roll out into either room.
5. Shelves for books and toys.

VIEW FROM ABOVE SHOWS THE UPPER-LEVEL SPACES.

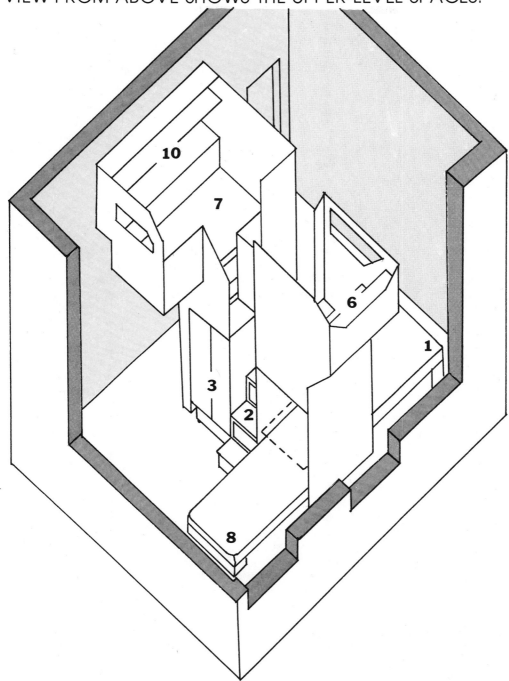

6. Upper-level desk area.
7. Upper-level play area doubles as loft bed.
8. Slide-out bed.
9. Fold-down desk.
10. Shelves for toys and books.

INDEX